HISTORICAL AND DESCRIPTIVE MEMOIR

ARCHITECTURE IN DHARWAR AND MYSORE

HISTORICAL AND DESCRIPTIVE MEMOIR

MEADOWS TAYLOR

Published by

Gyan Publishing House
5, Ansari Road
Daryaganj, New Delhi-110002
Phone: 011-47034999, 9811692060
E-mail: books@gyanbooks.com

Distribution Network
gyanbooks.com
India, USA, Canada, UK, Australia, France

ISBN : 978-81-212-3491-7 (PB)
First Published, 1866

2nd Impression 2020

Printed at: Gyan Press, Delhi.

Historical and Descriptive Memoir
Author: Meadows Taylor

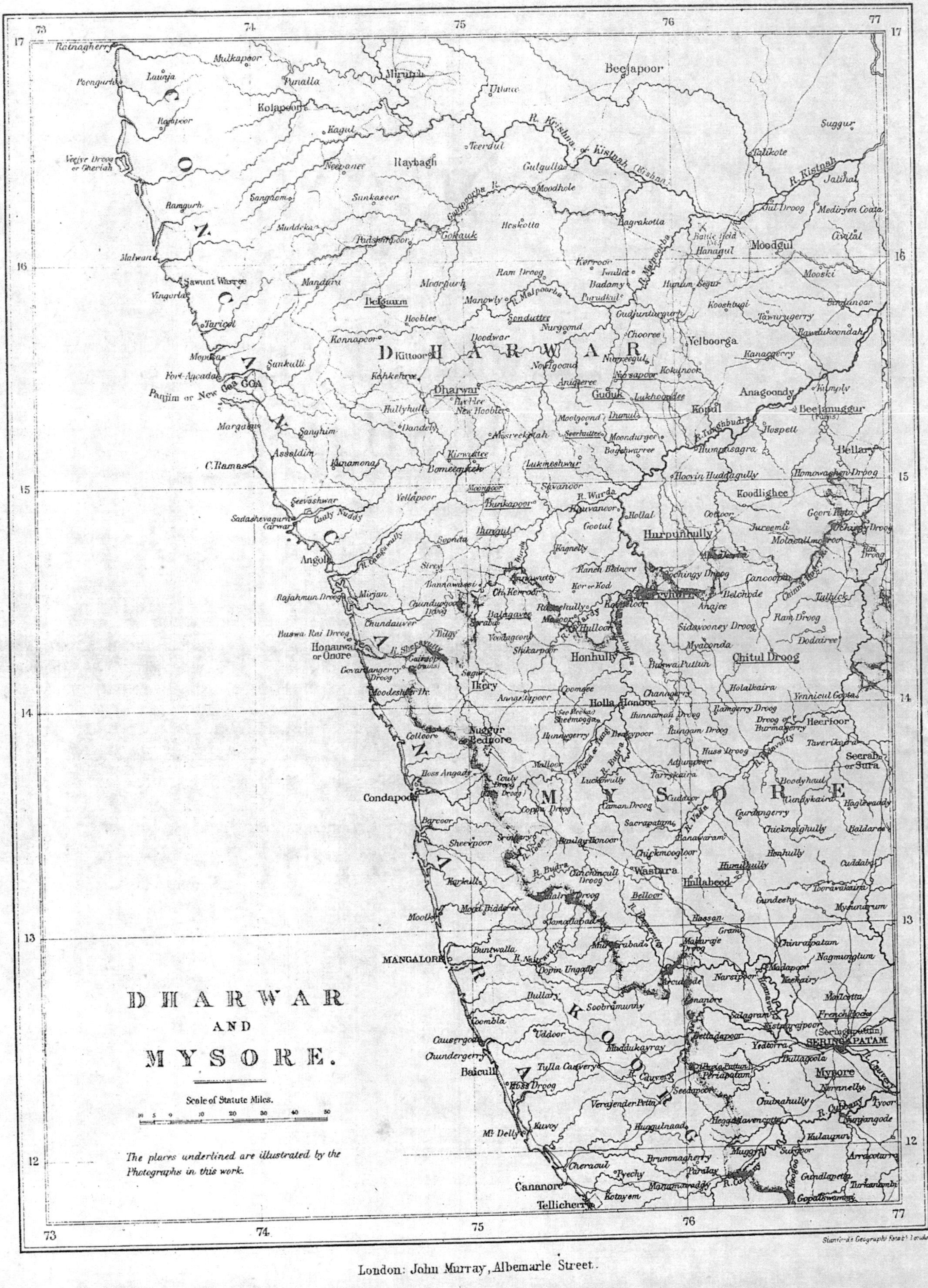

London: John Murray, Albemarle Street.

TO THE MEMORY OF

THE RIGHT HON. JOHN, LORD ELPHINSTONE, G.C.H., G.C.B.,

GOVERNOR OF BOMBAY,

UNDER WHOSE ENLIGHTENED ADMINISTRATION THE FIRST EFFORTS WERE MADE BY THE BRITISH GOVERNMENT

TO INTRODUCE TO EUROPE AND PERPETUATE, BY MEANS OF PHOTOGRAPHIC ART,

THE NOBLE MONUMENTS OF WESTERN INDIA,

This Volume

IS INSCRIBED, WITH DEEP REGRET AT THE PREMATURE CLOSE

OF HIS DISTINGUISHED CAREER.

CONTENTS.

HISTORICAL MEMOIR, BY COLONEL MEADOWS TAYLOR.

	Page
PART I. ON THE DYNASTIES OF THE CARNATIC ANTERIOR TO THE MAHOMEDAN INVASION	1
The Chalúkya Dynasty	2
The Kâla Bhuryas	6
The Yadava Dynasty of Deogurh	8
The Yadavas, surnamed Hoi Sala, or Bellâl	10
Of the Great Families of the Kuntala Des	11
PART II. OF THE WESTERN HINDOO DYNASTIES SUBSEQUENT TO THE MAHOMEDAN INVASION OF THE DECCAN	13
1. Vijaya nugger or Beejanuggur	13
Bukka and Harihara	15
Deva Raya	16
2. Mysore	27
3. Hurpunhullee and Chittuldroog	37

HISTORICAL MEMOIR,

By Colonel Meadows Taylor, M. R. I. A., F. G. S. I., Etc.

Part I.

ON THE DYNASTIES OF THE CARNATIC ANTERIOR TO THE MAHOMEDAN INVASION.

THE CARNATIC, or, according to ancient Hindoo geographers, Karnata Des, is that portion of the Peninsula of India in which the "Kanara," or Canarese, language has been the vernacular of the people from the earliest ages to which historical record extends. Time does not appear to have caused any limitation of its area, and though the language, like all others in India, has undergone some modifications of dialect, it is essentially the same now as it was a thousand years ago; not a derivative from the Sanscrit, but, like the Tamul, and other cognate southern languages, an original stock, which has been enriched and strengthened by Sanscrit in all that related to the expression of religious philosophy, science, art, poetry, or general literature. The boundaries of this language are necessarily irregular. They may be defined to the south by the plateau of Mysore, below and beyond which the Tamul language exists; to the east, by a line passing through Nundidroog, Penkonda, Adoni, Rachore, and Goolburgah, to Beeder, its most northern point; the Teloogoo, or Telinga language being spoken eastwards as far as the coast, and embracing an area nearly equal to that of the Canarese. To the north, by an irregular line passing from Beeder by Kulliani, Sholapoor, Punderpoor, Kurar, and Kolapoor, to Gheria, or Viziadroog, on the sea; the language to the north being Mahratta. The whole tract, therefore, comprises six degrees of latitude, 12° to 18°, and four degrees of longitude, 73½° to 77½°, forming an area of about 115,000 square miles, and containing at the present time from ten to twelve millions of inhabitants; nor is there any reason to believe that in the earliest periods of its authentic history, or for the last ten centuries, the population, in the aggregate, has fluctuated in any remarkable degree.

The remote periods of Hindoo settlement by Aryan tribes, in the north of India, have been traced with some degree of accuracy by antiquarian research; but no similar clue has, as yet, been obtained as to the settlement of the south, or the conversion of its people to the Hindoo faith. The most probable supposition on the latter point is, that Aryan Brahmins and Kshuttris accompanied Rama, King of Oude, in his invasion of the south of India, and Ceylon, which he conquered. To this day, the Mahratta language is termed in Canarese, "Arya Mát," or the Aryan tongue. At that period, though the central portion of the peninsula is represented to have been a forest, as it is to a great extent at present, the only inhabitants of which were wild men, giants, monkeys and demons; yet the south was emphatically a "junnusthan," or abode of men, and as intercourse of a peaceful kind ultimately ensued with them, it may be presumed they were already civilized to a great extent. After Rama's return to Oude, the desire of propagation of the Hindoo faith, as well as the acquisition of power, prompted many persons to follow in his steps; and thus the original invasion became the means of successive conquest and improvement. Among these new settlers were the chiefs who founded the Pandyan and Chola kingdoms, at what date it is impossible to discover or conjecture; nor is it until the records of Greece and Rome connect them with the West by descriptions, by trade, and even by treaties, that their existence can be traced appears doubtful, from the fact that Jainism was occasionally, perhaps, professed by some of them, and their return to orthodox Brahminism, recorded by inscriptions in learned Sanscrit. That the Jains existed, and in great prosperity for the most part, is proved by those costly and beautiful remains of their pious adoration which will be illustrated in this volume, and that Buddhists were tolerated also cannot either be doubted; but the latter had evidently dwindled to an obscure sect. Among the great works of the Chalúkyas are the cave temples at Khurosa, a village about twenty-five miles north-west from Kulliani, which are almost unknown. They are in the same style as those of Ellora, but the rock, a cellular trap and laterite, was not favourable for any finish, and most of them are incomplete. It is by no means improbable that some of the caves of Ellora, and in particular Kylas, which is entirely of a southern style of architecture, may have been the work of the Chalúkyas; but at Kulliani itself, except some curious excavated chambers in a small isolated hill, said to have been a monastery and college, and a great extent of shapeless mounds, nothing remarkable remains to prove the existence of the capital of a great dynasty, which had reigned over nearly half of the peninsula.

II. THE KALA BHURYAS.

IT may be interesting to the reader to know how the family of the Kála Bhuryas, which, under Vijala had usurped the larger portion of the Chalúkya kingdom, fared afterwards; and their history is well established by their inscriptions. The Kála Bhuryas were hereditary nobles of the Chalúkya kingdom, and, according to their genealogy, their ancestors had emigrated from Kalinga, in Hindostan. It will be remembered that mention of them is made in the Yeoor inscription as having been overcome by the Chalúkyas in the early period of the dynasty: and it does not seem at all improbable, from the tenacity with which Hindoos cling to ancestral traditions, that Vijala's usurpation was, in his eyes, and perhaps those of the people, justified by the existence of former family royalty. He was not, however, destined to found a new dynasty; and the circumstances that attended his death, the disruption of his family power, and the establishment of a new and popular faith, which has spread over the whole of the south-western portion of India, the professors of which may be reckoned by millions—are memorable events in the political, romantic, and religious history of the Carnatic, and are the subjects of innumerable poems, tales, historical legends, and sacred writings, now in daily use among the Lingayet sect as far as the limits of the Canarese language extends, and beyond that into Maharashtra and Telingana. The Lingayet sect is, in fact, the popular one of the south of India, embracing Sudras of all denominations, and far exceeding the Brahminical in the numbers of its votaries.

The person who was the originator of the sect, by name Busava, or popularly Bussappa, was a Brahmin, born of humble parents, in the village of Bagawadi in the present Talook or division of Moodébihal, of the Sholapoor collectorate: though by some the village of Ingleshwur is said to have been his birth-place. By his great progress in learning, and his disputations in company with his father Mahdu Bhutt, a Sivaic Brahmin, he soon attracted notice, and resorted to the metropolis of the kingdom, Kulliani, then ruled by Vijala Kálabhúri. There he rose rapidly, and married the daughter of Vijala's prime minister. Bussappa had a sister, named Pudmawati, who was extremely beautiful; and the King Vijala having seen her, became enamoured of her, and, though he was a Jain and she a Brahmin, married her. Under this connection, Bussappa became Danda Nayk, or commander in chief of the royal armies; and so adroitly exercised the power he had gained through his sister, that the king gave up all executive authority to him. The usual result followed. Bussappa strengthened his position by appointing his own creatures to all the high offices of the state, yet without alarming the king. When he had gained this elevated position, however, he began to disseminate a new creed, which, as his votaries believe, he had adopted in his youth, in consequence of a special divine revelation. It rejected caste, and all idol worship except the phallic emblems of creation as illustrative of one God, which were to be borne about the person, and was thus termed "Jungam," or peripatetic: and the priests of the new creed were called after them Jungamas. In some respects, the Jungam creed held a mid-way position between the rival faiths of the Brahmins and the Jains, but differed in essential points from both; the same observance of abstinence from animal food was enjoined; but the rituals were simpler, more devotional, and more easy of comprehension by the lower orders of the people. Parts of the Poorans, and of the Vedas also were selected as orthodox, the rest rejected ; and finally Bussappa assumed the position of an incarnation of Nundi, the bull of Siva, and was acknowledged to be an apostle of the Divinity, with a sacred message to men.

Vijala was now alarmed, and sought to destroy his minister ; but Bussappa escaped. He was pursued, however; and being joined by partisans, routed a detachment of the royal troops. Vijala now took command in person; and Bussappa, who by this time was at the head of a vast horde of converts, met the king in the field, and defeated him with great loss: but immediately afterwards tendering his allegiance, accompanied him to Kulliani, and was reinstated in his ministerial honours. Henceforward Bussappa's main object was to secure the succession to the throne for his sister's child, Veer Vijala ; and there can be little doubt that the king was assassinated, though many local legends declare that he abdicated and became an ascetic, delivering over the kingdom to Bussappa as regent for his son. Whether by assassination, of which several accounts are given in the "Buswa Poorans," or legendary histories, or after abdication, Vijala's death occurred S. 1088, A.D. 1166, nine years after his usurpation of the Chalúkya kingdom. The young Rajah, however, did not allow his father's murder to rest unrevenged, and Bussappa was obliged once more to fly from Kulliani. He was pursued to Virishapoora on the Malabar coast by his prince, and, to escape capture and torture, committed suicide by drowning himself in a well. His body was found and ignominiously cast out to be devoured by wild beasts; and the name of the town was changed, perhaps ironically, to "Ulave," or, as it may be called, the "sanctuary," though it did not prove the sanctuary Bussappa had hoped for. This is the Jain account of the end of this remarkable character. The Lingayets, while they cannot deny that the young prince desired to revenge his father's death, and that Bussappa fled from Kulliani, believe that he was miraculously absorbed into the divinity as he sat praying upon a stone "lingam," opposite to the image of a sacred "nanda," or bull, in the temple of Sungmeshwur, at the junction of the Malpurba and Krishna rivers, when the stone opened, and he disappeared beneath it ; an inequality in the stone is believed to mark the place, which, as well as Ulave, is resorted to by thousands of pilgrims.

The fate of Bussappa did not deter the progress of the Lingayet faith, indeed may be said to have strengthened and advanced its promulgation. Its converts in a short time could be counted by hundreds of thousands, and the nephew of its originator, Chun Bussappa, the son of another sister, proved to be an able and successful apostle, meeting Brahmin and Jain priests in public controversies, and proving victor in them ; these acts, as related in his history, being accompanied by many miracles, which have unbounded credence. In the village of Arlagoondagi, of the Shorapoor district, some lineal descendants of Chun Bussappa still live, and have in their possession many relics of him which are held in the highest veneration. The cradle in which he slept, some of his clothes, his drinking vessel, and the silver box hung round his neck which contained the emblems of his belief, are interesting memorials, at the distance of seven hundred years, to the followers of the faith he propagated, which prevails over a far greater extent of country and variety of population than ever perhaps was contemplated by its founder.

Although the records of this dynasty extend to an early period, that of the fifth century, it may be inferred from the style of the inscriptions, the political transactions, and probably of the architecture, that the Chalúkya kingdom was at least as civilized as that of the Pandoos or the Cholas of the south; that the state of society admitted of the existence of social communities; of district colleges and religious edifices; of the control of laws, and recognition of property in land; that there were hereditary public offices, places of guild and trade, and general commerce. Nor indeed can there be much doubt that, from their seaports in the west, the Chalúkyas traded with the Arabs, Greeks, and Romans, who may have penetrated even to their capital. The names of villages do not appear to have changed since that period, and Yeoor, Nagavi, Sirála (Sirwal), Malkheir, and many others, given as localities of inscriptions by Mr. Walter Elliott, still exist in His Highness the Nizam's, the Shorapoor, and the British territory. Indeed, there is little reason to believe either that the population, the agriculture, or the style of the villages of these provinces, has altered in any considerable degree for the last fifteen hundred years.

THE YADAVA DYNASTY OF DEVAGIRI, OR DEOGURH.

OF the Yádavas two separate families can be traced bearing the same name, the one ruling partly over the Deccan proper, with a portion of the Carnatic conquered from the Chalúkyas; the other, over provinces lying to the south west of the Chalúkya dominions, which bore the distinctive appellation of "Bellal." The first of these follows the Chalúkyas in order, and the interval of 128 years which succeeded the disruption of this kingdom and the death of Vijala Kálabhurya in S. 1088, A.D. 1166, to the Mahomedan invasion of Alla-oo-Deen in A.D. 1294, was the greatest of their power. Several inscriptions quoted by Mr. Walter Elliot give the genealogy of the eldest branch of the family from the earliest presumed ancestor, which will be noticed in its proper place. There are comparatively few inscription records of the Devagiri branch of the family, and the period at which they separated from the elder stock is not discoverable. The earliest date ascertained is found in an inscription of Ballam Deva at Hippergah in the Sholapoor collectorate. which is twenty-four years subsequent to the acquisition of the Chalúkya kingdom, and is of S. 1112, A.D. 1190. It contains vague enumerations of dynasties to the following effect:—"First reigned the mighty race of Pandu; "and after them came many others . . . of the Surya Vansa, became illustrious; . . . . the "Chalúkyas, many of whom having reigned with power were overthrown; and the race of Kala-bhurya "Bijala obtained celebrity by the strength of their arms, and reigned for a time; after which the splendour of "the Yadu Kula became conspicuous, like that of Bhima." Traces of the conquests of the Yadus are found for the most part in inscriptions in the present Dharwar district, and prove them to have extended over the whole of the western and south western provinces of the Chalúkyas; and it appears from these records, that not only the Chalúkya, but the Bellál kingdom, the capital of which was Dwara Samoodra, in Mysore, had also succumbed to them. These conquests were made by Sinha Deva, who succeeded his grandfather Ballam Deva in S. 1132, A.D. 1220; and the acquisition of Vulara or Malabar, and the Konkan, by his general Bomma Deva, is especially commemorated. The last of his inscriptions is dated S. 1169, A.D. 1247, when he had reigned thirty years, residing at Devagiri, or Deogurh. Two other successors follow, Kunner Deva in S. 1170, A.D. 1248, and Mahadeva in S. 1182, A.D. 1260. The last independent prince was Mahadeva's son, Ramchunder, who succeeded his father in S. 1193, A.D. 1271, and under the name of "Ram Deo," was the first to encounter the Mahomedans under Alla-oo-Deen Khiljy in S. 1216, A.D. 1294.

Against this new and warlike power, the Hindoo princes of the Deccan made comparatively little resistance; and the hardy Moghul and Tartar veterans seem to have borne down all before them. At Ellichpoor in Berar, Alla-oo-Deen fought his first action with the Hindoos of the south, and a great mound near the city bearing the legend of the "Gunj Shaheed," "the heap of martyrs," commemorates those who were slain on this occasion. It is not improbable, perhaps, that the action was a severe one; but it was decisive, for between Ellichpoor and Deogurh the young invader met with no opposition. On his arrival there, according to Ferishta's record, he invested the place, the fortifications of which were not then complete. The Rajah and his son were both absent; but the former returning with all speed, strove to throw himself between the city and the enemy, and in doing so suffered a severe defeat. This is probably the most authentic account; but another assigns the Rajah's submission to the fact of a large number of sacks of salt having been taken into the fort, by mistake, instead of flour; on the discovery of which, there being no other provision left, capitulation became inevitable. Meanwhile his son, Shunkur Déva, who had collected an army, attacked Alla-oo-Deen, in defiance of his father's request to the contrary, and being utterly overthrown, Rama Déva was obliged to submit to enormous terms of ransom, which are scarcely credible—600 maunds of pearls, two maunds of jewels, 1000 of silver, 4000 pieces of silk, and other precious commodities are enumerated as the victor's spoils; and, perhaps, greatest of all, the engagement of the Rajah to pay an annual tribute to Dehli. It may easily be supposed that such a booty excited the cupidity of the northern Mahomedans to the highest pitch: and the comparatively easy manner in which it had been obtained, combined with the knowledge of even greater Hindoo kingdoms to the south, ripe for plunder, rendered any long inaction impossible. For a time the tribute was remitted to Dehli; but on its failure, a great army of 100,000 horse, under Mullik Kafoor, an enterprising general, was dispatched to the south. This occurred in S. 1228, A.D. 1306, twelve years after the first invasion, when very probably the Hindoos had ceased to apprehend further molestation. It was on this occasion that the beautiful Dewul Ranee, daughter of the Rajah of Goozerat, who was on her way to Deogurh to be married to the son of the Yadu Rajah, fell into the hands of a Mahomedan detachment, and was sent to Dehli, where she was married to King Alla-oo-Deen's son, Khizr Khan. The king's wife, Kowla Devi, had been the wife of Dewul Ranee's father, and one of the objects of the expedition was to bring away the young princess. Under other circumstances this might have been impossible; but the nuptial party, proceeding to Deogurh, was met by chance near the caves of Ellora by part of the advanced guard of Mullik Kafoor's army, and a skirmish ensued, in which the princess's horse was wounded by an arrow and fell, and her capture followed. This romantic event was celebrated by a Persian poem of much tenderness and beauty, which is still in existence. Ràma Deva did not long hold out against the Mahomedans, who, leaving a portion of their army to invest Deogurh, rapidly overran the country. On Mullik Kafoor's return he accompanied him to Dehli where he was hospitably received and entertained, and dismissed with honour and respect. This kindness probably influenced his future life, for the tribute to Dehli was regularly paid, and in S. 1231, A.D. 1309, he entertained Mullik Kafoor, on his return from the north, and accompanied him to his frontier at Indoor, near Beeder, on his march against the kingdom of Wurungol. On the Rajah's return to Deogurh he died, and was succeeded by his son Shunkul, or Shunker, Deva.

This prince may be considered the last of the Yadava dynasty. He was by no means of the same accommodating or submissive spirit as his father, and by his haughty contempt of, and resistance to, the Mahomedans, brought their whole power against his kingdom. In 1310, Mullik Kafoor returned to Deogurh on his march southwards to Dwara Samoodra, and was indifferently received by the Rajah; but nothing hostile occurred till 1312, when Shunkul Deva having withheld his tribute, Mullik Kafoor attacked and defeated him. On this occasion Shunkul Deva was seized and put to death, and the whole of his kingdom—"from the ports of Dabul and Chaul to Rachore and Moodgul"—annexed to the empire of Dehli. During the troublous times of the Mahomedan Empire which followed the acquisition of the Deccan, Hurpal Deva, brother-in-law of Shunkul Deva, made a gallant effort to recover the kingdom: and at the period of the Emperor Alla-oo-Deen's death, in A.D. 1316, had wrested many provinces from the Mahomedans; but two years afterwards his son, Moobarak Khilji, marched in person to the Deccan, when Hurpàl Deva fled, was captured, flayed alive, and decapitated by this cruel tyrant, and his head stuck on the gate of Deogurh. Thus fell the last of the great Yadava princes. The remainder of the family retired to estates in the fastnesses of the western Ghâts, and never again attempted resistance; they are now represented by the Jadows of the Mahratta Deccan, a numerous and respectable family. The history of their capital after the death of Hurpàl belongs to that of the Mahomedans in the Deccan, with which this memoir has no concern.

The dominions of the Yádavas extended from the Nerbudda, or at least the Tapty, to the north, westwards to the sea at the ports of Dabul and Chaul, and to the east and south from Berar to Indoor, near Beeder, and thence probably, in nearly a direct line, to the Tumboodra river and the sea. When they had overcome the Bellal Yádavas of Dwara Samoodra, their frontier probably met that of the Chola Rajahs of Kunchi, in the present Mysore country, if indeed they did not possess the plateau as far as its southern edge. This extent of territory is very great, and the dynasty must have been one of the wealthiest of the southern Hindoos; but the remains of it now existent are comparatively very few. It is possible that the earlier princes may have created the curious fort of Devagiri, or Deogurh, and made it their capital; and it is certainly one of the most remarkable works in India,—a large isolated hill upwards of 500 feet high and upwards of a mile in circumference having been scarped all round through solid trap rock to the height of 120 to 150 feet perpendicular from the ground, leaving a wide, deep ditch; access to the top being through a tunnel excavated in the centre of the hill. But other dynasties, preceding and succeeding Shálivâhana, anterior to the Christian era, are perhaps the more likely authors of this great work; nor is it at all inconsistent with the geographical position assumed by Ptolemy, that Deogurh, or the remains of that city which existed on the table-land between the fort and the caves of Ellora, may have been the Tagara or the Plithana which are named in the Periplus, and were assuredly places of trade and consequence in the Deccan at the period of his existence. Antiquarians have been unable, hitherto, to determine the exact positions of these places; but for many concurrent reasons, which need not be detailed here, the inference in favour of the ancient city near Deogurh is supported by the fact that Grecian and Roman coins have been found there. Mr. Elphinstone assumes that Ptolemy's Plithana, ΠΛΙΘΑΝΑ, is no more than Paithana, ΠΑΙΘΑΝΑ, the orthographic error being evident; and there is a Paitan on the Godavery which is supposed to have been the capital of Shálivàhana in the first century. As reasonably, however, it may be assumed that Tagara, τάγαρα, is an orthographical error for Nagara, ναγαρα (?) In this case, as Paithana and Nagara have precisely the same signification of "city," they may have originally meant one and the same piace, which in reality was the ancient "city" already mentioned; and it is consistent with the splendid era of Shálivàhana that he should not only have carved out the fort of Deogurh, but Hinduized the Buddhist caves of Ellora, adding others of his own to the already existing series. To these, however, the Temple of Kylas must be an exception; its architectural style is unquestionably that of southern India, and the general design and ornamental portions of the pillars correspond with many of the temples of Mysore and the southern Mahratta country, which will be illustrated in this volume, and were erected probably between the sixth and thirteenth centuries.

OF THE YADAVAS, SURNAMED HOI SALA, OR BELLÁL.

OF this dynasty there are traces by inscriptions both in the Mackenzie and Elliot collections, and the legend of the rise of the family is the same in both. A "Sala" progenitor resided in Sasakapura. In the gardens of that town dwelt a Brahpate, or Yoti, who, when sitting in "tapassa," or meditation, was attacked by a tiger, Puli, or Shardúla, a fearful beast with dreadful eyes, and lashing its sides with its tail. The devotee gave Sala a weapon, blessed it, and said, "Saladu poi" (draw and kill); on which he drew the weapon and killed the tiger, and hence the appellation Poi Sala, or Hoi Sala. Other traditions allege that Sala slew the tiger, which was committing great depredations, at the request of the villagers, who thenceforward allowed him annually "a quarter of a fanam on every candy of their grain crops, with which he raised "adherents and became formidable, increasing his demands in proportion to his success, till his revenue reached "fourteen fanams on every candy." Sala, in any case, became the founder of the greatness of the family, and assumed the title of "Belláia," from his power (Bala), and adopted the tiger, or Shardúla, as his family ensign. A genealogy, quoted by Mr. Walter Elliot from several inscriptions, gives a list of eight princes, the last of whom is Narasinha, who is described as ruling from his own limits to Uchangi Dargah, and laving his horses sides in the Krishna. The actual boundary to the north, therefore, being Uchangi, not far from the present Hurpunhullee, the rest may be understood as conveying an idea of the limits of the predatory raids; and as the Chalúkyas unquestionably ruled as far as the Tumboodra, the inference that the Bellálas pressed their conquests as far as the Krishna cannot be maintained. It has already been noticed, also, that in the reign of Vikram Chalúkya II, the Bellálas were defeated in an invasion of the Chalúkya kingdom by Achuga Devi, the Chalúkya general. Vishnuverddhana, or Bitti Deva, the Bellál king, unquestionably the greatest of the dynasty, who made this invasion, was the fifth prince in succession to Sala, and cotemporary of Vikram Chalúkya II: and, as Mr. Walter Elliot observes, may have penetrated to the Krishna before he was defeated. The local tradition, indeed, before alluded to, fixes the scene of the great battle near Moodgul, in the Rachore Dooab. The grandson of this king, by name Veer Belláia, who succeeded after two intermediate princes, Udayaditya, and Narasinha I, appears to have been a warlike person, who extended the Bellál dominions not only north of the Tumboodra, that is, probably into the Rachore Dooab, but over the whole of the southern Mahratta country or Canara, called Kuntala Des; and it is recorded in the inscription at Guduk, that his general, Bomma, defeated the army of the Kálabhuryas, commanded by Brahma Chamupati, capturing sixty elephants; moreover, that he destroyed the "ships" of the southern country. These events would seem to fix the era of his dynasty at the period of the final dissolution of the Chalúkya kingdom under Vijala. In the record of the Devagiri Yádava, "Ballam," at Hippergah, S. 1112, A.D. 1190 (ante), a victory is claimed over the Bellàls; and it is by no means improbable that both parties engaged may have claimed and recorded advantages which neither absolutely gained. Be this as it may, there is no doubt that the war between the Yádavas of Devagiri, Deogurh, and the Bellálas, continued for some time; and by an inscription at Anigiri, it is recorded that in a great battle in which Ballam was pursued from Surtur to Lokigonda, he was slain by Veer Bellál himself. Mr. Walter Elliot gives a translation of this event from the inscription, which is an interesting record:—

"Boasting of his elephants, his horses, and his men, Balam Nrapa exclaimed, 'Who dare oppose me?' "Belál, mounting his single elephant, urged it onwards, and trampling down his army, pursued him and slew "him, chasing him from Surtur to Lokigonda," &c. After this, or probably about this period, the royal residence was removed from Dwâra Samoodra to Lokigonda, now Lukhoondee, near Dumbal, or it may have been the northern capital only; and at Hookoor on the Tumboodra, Mr. Walter Elliot found traces of an immense encampment, with erect stones to which elephants or horses were fastened. This prince reigned from S. 1114, A.D. 1192, to S. 1133, A.D 1211, and the locality of his grants, for which inscriptions exist, is confined to the area between the Malpurba and the Tumboodra, a very limited space certainly: but it may be assumed that in those distracted times of almost constant war, the Bellál prince, finding no molestation from the southern kingdom of Chola, preferred to watch the movements of the Devagiri Yádavas from the northern portion of his own frontier. Of his son Narasinha II. only one inscription is mentioned by Mr. Walter Elliot, which is at Hungul, and relates to transactions to the southwards. Nor are there any records of succession after Narasinha. The resistance and defence made by Veer Bellál against the Devagiri Yádavas was not continued by Narasinha, for Sinha Déva, of Devagiri, grandson of Ballam, obtained a great victory over the Belláls, "rooting up the power "of the 'Hoisála,' 'Bellála,' &c, and again, as has been quoted (*ante*), his general Hôn Bômma, governor of Nul-"goond, presented his prince with fourteen elephants, the best of the spoil which he had taken with great bravery "from Narasimha Nrassa." In these transactions the dates of the Bellála and Yádava record-inscriptions confirm each other in a remarkable manner. Dwara Samoodra, the capital of the Bellálas, was in possession of the family in S. 1294, A.D. 1310, when Mullik Kafoor and Khwaja Hajy marched southwards, "where they heard there "were temples very rich in gold and jewels." "Among others," writes Ferishta, "they engaged Bilál (Bellál) Déo, "Rajah of the Carnatic, and, defeating him, took him prisoner and ravaged his territory. They found in the "temples prodigious spoils, such as idols of gold adorned with precious stones, and other rich effects, consecrated to "Hindoo worship." The city of Dwara Samoodra was built in A.D. 1133, according to a poem quoted by Colonel Wilks, and as it was destroyed in 1310, it had existed 177 years, which probably marks the reign of the most powerful period of the dynasty. How the family in their reduced circumstances existed in after times there is no record: but it may be inferred that for a while it remained a feudatory of the Beejanuggur kingdom; for Colonel Wilks records that a branch of it was allowed to exercise a nominal authority at "Tonoor" until A.D. 1387. Tonoor, ten miles from Seringapatam, was then one of the provinces of the ancient Bellál kingdom, all others northward having been gradually absorbed by the kings of Beejanuggur; and in this obscurity the Bellál dynasty, eventually absorbed by that of Beejanuggur, became extinct. At the best period of its existence the princes of the Bellála dynasty were Jains, which may account for the number of beautiful temples which remain monuments of their sway. That at their capital of Dwara Samoodra in particular, which is Hindoo, and marks the period of the dynastic change of faith, will be illustrated in the present volume.

OF THE GREAT FAMILIES OF THE KUNTALA DES.

THE acknowledged Hindoo dynasties anterior to the Mahomedan invasion of the country, of which the pictorial illustrations of this volume exist, have been traced in order; and it remains only to mention those great hereditary feudatories, or semi-independent chieftains, who existed contemporaneously, and to whom, especially those who professed the Jain faith, most of the ancient temples, wells, tanks, and other great public works, are to be attributed; they are not, however, numerous. Inscriptions relating to four only are quoted in the Elliot collection; but these are, no doubt, of the most powerful families, who were attached to, or dependent upon, the great Chalúkya dynasty. The first in rank of these were the Kálabhuryas, who have been before noticed; but besides the branch which finally subverted the Chalúkyas, there was another whose estate or principality seems to have been on the Malpurbah river, near Rône. The inscriptions, however, are merely grants, and, with the family, have no particular historical interest.

The Silharas were Mahá Mundleshwurs, or nobles, of the highest rank in the Chalúkya kingdom, whose possessions lay at and about Kolapoor. The inscriptions in which their genealogies are enumerated are dated S. 1057, A.D. 1135, and S 1065, A.D. 1143, and give a list of twelve heads of the family, up to the founder, Amarindra Silhara; but his era is not stated. Mr. Walter Elliot conjectures that the last expedition of Vijala Kálabhurya, the usurper of Kulyan, was against this family. Of this event the Vijala chronicle records, that the king, "warned in a dream of his approaching death," summoned all the nobles of the kingdom, and all having attended except the Silharas, he marched against them; and after some negotiation on the Bheema river, continued his journey to Kolapoor, which he besieged, and having breached the wall, "Suri Danda" Natha submitted. One of the appellations of this family, "Tagara Pur," has excited much interest, and great endeavours have been made to throw light upon it; but the inscriptions give no clue as to where Tagara, whence they had their origin, actually was. If, however, Deogurh was in reality the Tagara of a very ancient date, many families of note may have sprung either from the local dynasty, or its nobility, at the period of the disruption of its dominions. No inscription of the Silharas has been discovered later than S. 1137, A.D. 1215, and it is most probable that the family disappeared in the subsequent troublous times.

Kadamba is a third noble family, of which their inscriptions give an unbroken genealogy of fifteen successions from Mayura Varma Deva I. to Mayura Varma Deva II, S. 956, A.D. 1034. The date of the earliest is not given; but Mr. Walter Elliot assumes that, allowing thirty years to a generation, the era may be S. 500 or 550, A.D. 578 or 628, which would raise it to an equality of descent with the Chalúkyas,—a supposition by no means, perhaps, improbable. The hereditary possessions of this family were in the province of Banawassee, and their tenure of them is believed to have been anterior to the establishment of the Chalúkyas, and contemporary with the Rattas and Silharas. To the originator of the family, Mayura Varma, is attributed the introduction of Brahmins, and the Hindoo, or Brahminical faith, into the province; but at what date it is impossible to conjecture. That they were subject to and servants of the Chalúkyas appears from several inscriptions dated S. 956, 969, 997, the incumbent holding his office of Governor of Banawassee, &c, by appointment of Bhunéka Malla Chalúkya. Of this family Dr. Buchanan obtained some interesting records in Malabar, proving that their dominions extended to the sea coast at one period, and embraced much of Malabar and the southern Concan. It is most probable, therefore, that when the Chalúkyas prevailed over them, they became feudatories of portions of their original possessions.

The Rattas have been mentioned before as for a time successful over the Chalúkyas, and being afterwards subdued by them in turn; Jaya Sinha Chalúkya, according to the Yeoor inscription, "overcame the army "of 800 elephants of the son of the Moon Ratta Kula, named Krishta. He destroyed that prince, with "his army of 500 elephants; thus the goddess of royalty was attained by the Chalúkya race." The Rattas were Jains, and were lords of Samditi, near Pursghur, and local inscriptions attest their existence up to S. 1019, A.D. 1097; another branch, or probably the same family, governed at Gutal, on the Tumboodra; a third at Pattudkul, near Badami, and at Belgavé, under Ramchundra Yádu, of Devagiri, bringing the existence of the family nearly to the Mahomedan conquest, at which time they were probably in possession of those ancestral offices which seem to have been analogous to the modern Nargowras, or Deshmookhs.

During the whole of the period in which these families and their superior dynasties existed, that is, from the fifth to the twelfth and thirteenth centuries of the Christian era, the Carnatic, and in particular that portion of it named Kuntala Des, seems to have been prosperous and advancing in civilization. It was well cultivated and covered with villages, as it is at present; and the fertility of its soil, and probably the facilities it possessed of trade with the coast, and export of its manufactures and productions to Egypt and to Arabia, through Greek, Roman, and Arabian merchants, no doubt formed a national element of its prosperity, of which its beautiful architectural remains are to the present day indisputable proofs. To a great extent the Jain religion prevailed over the Brahminical up to the sixth and seventh centuries and wherever it prospered, as in Guzerat, the most elaborate and exquisitely finished temples were erected by its votaries; but neither were the Brahmins idle, for their representative edifices are met with as frequently as those of the Jains. In short, from Dwára Samoodra, now Hullabeed, in Mysore, northwards to Kolapoor, and from the Tumboodra to the Ghauts, there are few villages in which there are not examples of the architectural skill, the taste, and the wonderfully elaborate execution of the stone edifices of that period, of which the illustrations to this volume will afford the reader ample confirmation. The period referred to, the fifth to the tenth century, it will be remembered, is that from the evacuation of Britain by the Romans to the end of the Saxon dynasties; and its remains in India prove the unquestionable superiority of the eastern over the western skill in decorative architecture.

PART II.

OF THE WESTERN HINDOO DYNASTIES SUBSEQUENT TO THE MAHOMEDAN INVASION OF THE DECCAN.

I. VIJAYA NUGGUR OR BEEJANUGGUR.

CONSEQUENT upon the subversion of the Chalúkya dynasty by the Yádavas, and their probably insecure possession of their southern and western conquests under the incursions of the Bellál princes of Dwára Samoodra, it will have been evident that the provinces lying between the Krishna river and the line of Ghauts, can hardly have belonged to a permanent government for any length of time; and a number of small states, principalities, or petty baronies arose, and maintained existence. On the subversion of the Yádavas by the Mahomedans, and Mullik Kafoor's progress as far as Dwára Samoodra, in 1310, when the Bellál dynasty was either extinguished or driven farther to the south, it seems very questionable whether the Mahomedans attempted to retain the whole of the country which had fallen before their arms. Such a course would have been manifestly impossible from their great distance from bases of support; and even in the fourth expedition of Mullik Kafoor, in A. D. 1312, he had not established the Imperial authority to a further line southwards than the Krishna, or at most the Tumboodra. Ferishta records that, after the execution of the Rajah of Déogurh, Mullik Kafoor laid waste the countries of "Maharashtra and Canara, from Dabul and "Choul—which are ports on the western coast—as far as Rachore and Moodgul:" and though he probably held Belgaum and Goa, and the provinces north of them, and of a line from Belgaum to the confluence of the Krishna and Tumboodra which afterwards became the frontier of the Bahmuny dynasty,—yet all to the south of that line as yet, no doubt, belonged to the Hindoos.

In the year A. D. 1303 the first expedition against Wurungol was dispatched from Dehli, by the Emperor Alla-oo-Deen Khiljy, by the eastern route of Bengal. It was unsuccessful, and had been obliged to retreat in great distress. In 1309, therefore, another expedition was sent by way of Deogurh, under the command of Mullik Kafoor. Wurungul was besieged, and, after a gallant defence of several months, was at last taken by assault. The Rajah purchased peace by a large payment of treasure and other valuables, and having agreed to pay tribute to the Emperor, was left in possession of his dominions. This expedition occurs between Mullik Kafoor's second visit to Déogurh, and the first to Dwára Samoodra; and proves that the movements of the Moghul armies of that period, which appear to have been entirely composed of cavalry, were extremely rapid and vigorous. While Mullik Kafoor continued to reside at Déogurh, and, indeed, for several years, the Rajahs of Wurungul seem to have paid their tribute regularly, and to have been exempt from molestation by the Mahomedans; but taking advantage of the confusion which existed at Dehli after the death of Alla-oo-Deen, and through the disturbed reigns of Osman and Moobaruk Khiljy, to the accession of the Toghluk dynasty, the Prince of Wurungul had refused payment of tribute, and his country was again invaded, in A. D. 1332, by the Moghuls, under the Prince Aluf Khan Toghluk. On this occasion, partly owing to quarrels among themselves, and partly to the effects of climate, the Mahomedans were obliged to raise the siege, and were followed in their retreat to Déogurh, with much success, by the Rajah's forces. It is related that of all his great army, the Prince brought only 3000 horse back to Dehli; nevertheless, he was not long inactive. In the course of two months he had recruited his forces, and again marched upon Wurungul. On this occasion, the Prince occupied the fortified positions of the country as he advanced: Beeder, Kowlas, Indoor, and other strong fortresses fell in succession; and finally Wurungul was invested, and, on this occasion, captured. The Rajah, Luddur Deo, with all his family, were sent as prisoners to Dehli, and, for the time, the Andra dynasty was subverted. Telingana, which included all the dominions of the Wurungul princes, became a Mahomedan province, and the name of the capital was changed to Sooltanpoor. The Rajahs of Wurungul subsequently recovered the greater part of their dominions, and continued to enjoy them up to the disruption of the Bahmuny dynasty of Beeder, in 1489; but with this part of the history of the period the present memoir has no direct concern. It was necessary, however, to account for the destruction of Wurungul in 1322, to trace the imputed establishment of a new dynasty of the same family at Beejanuggur in A. D. 1366.

The period indeed was a propitious one. Mahomed Toghluk, Emperor of Dehli, was organizing expeditions to subdue China and Tartary, and indulging in wild dreams of the conquest of the eastern world. His Deccan and Telingana provinces were for the most part tranquil, and his local officers did not appear to desire to press their conquests more to the south. The acquisition of the newest portion of them, Telingana, had not proved so easy as that of the Deccan; the population was more warlike, and there were greater numbers of feudatories to subdue; in this direction, therefore, large numbers of the Imperial troops found occupation, and expeditions to the south became impossible. It can hardly be supposed that the Mahomedans had complete authority over the country south of the Krishna, or they would have noticed, and endeavoured to prevent, the establishment of a new and powerful Hindoo dynasty on the Tumboodra—their *presumed* southern boundary: but though Mullik Kafoor may have established posts as far as Moodgul and Rachore, the southern portion of the Dooab remained a disputed territory, while indeed, up to the fall of the Beejanuggur dynasty, the whole of the Rachore Dooab was a perpetual battle-field between the Hindoos and the Mahomedans, being alternately in possession of both, and in some instances divided between them.

The family of Beejanuggur claimed a very remote origin; and in a genealogy supplied to Mr. E. C. Ravenshaw, of the Bengal Civil Service, in 1829, by the Rajah of Anagoondi, which is published with an historical memoir in vol. xx. of the "Asiatic Researches," a list of eighty-five princes is given from Pandu, the attributed founder, to Yéshú Nandi, whose fourteen sons reigned over portions of his dominions. They were invaded by Amitra and Durmitra, from whence is not stated, and being conquered, fled to Telingana, where Nanda Mahárajah established the dynasty of Wurungul. This prince, after a reign of forty-two years, died in S. 998, A.D. 1076, and was succeeded by his son Chalik Rajah, who reigned forty-one years, and was succeeded by Vijala Raya, who reigned at Kulyan in S. 1041, A.D. 1119. Another son, Vijya Raya, established himself in the capital, Vijya Nuggur, in S. 1039-40, A.D. 1118, and from him descended four princes, the last of whom, Bhoop Raya, having no issue, Bukka Raya, the son of a neighbouring Rajah, perhaps of Kumply, which was a small independent State, was elevated to the Guddee in S. 1236, A.D. 1334. By this genealogy, the foundation of the Beejanuggur kingdom is traced to Vijala the last prince who reigned at Kulliani, and who, it will be remembered, had usurped the throne from the Chalúkya family. But Vijala had only one son; and whether he, after the conquest of his dominions by the Yadavas of Déogurh, established himself at Beejanuggur, and so founded a new dynasty there, or whether Bukka was a member of the Wurungul family who, escaping from the Mahomedans after their conquest of that city, rallied the dependants of his family around him, and established himself at Beejanuggur, is a doubtful point, which the genealogies and inscriptions of the family do not clear up. It is certainly against the assumption of any great antiquity for this family, that no traces of it by inscriptions are found in Mr. Walter Elliot's or Dr. Buchanan's collections; consequently it could not have existed as a reigning dynasty at the same period as the Chalúkyas, Bellâls, or Yádavas; nor, indeed, anterior to them, without leaving some memorial records which would have transpired.

Mr. H. H. Wilson, in his introductory memoir to the Mackenzie collection of inscriptions, while he details the foundation of the city of Beejanuggur by "Bukka and Harihara" in the beginning of the fourteenth century, does not attempt to trace their origin, except as fugitives from the kingdom of Wurungul, who, having met the great Brahmin missionary Mahdava, or Mahadeo Acharya, in the woods near Vijya Nuggur which he had founded, were appointed Rajahs by him. Mahadava Acharya himself gives evidence in his works on this point which can hardly be questioned, and is of far greater value than mere tradition. He states that he was the minister of Sangama the son of Kampa, a powerful prince whose rule extended to the southern, eastern, and western seas. Bukka and Harihara are the sons of Sangama; and one of their inscriptions (*vide* vol. ix. of the "Asiatic Researches") verifies Mahdava Acharya's chronicle. This account tallies also with that given by Ferishta at a later period, when the Hindoo dynasty is said to have lasted 700 years. Ferishta, however, in respect to Beejanuggur, does not seem able to avoid inconsistency, for in his history of the reign of Mahomed Toghluk, he records that, in 1344, Krishn Naik, son of Luddur Deo of Wurungul, went to Bilál Deo, Rajah of the Carnatic, and entered into a compact with him to oppose the Mahomedans. Bilál Deo agreed to join this combination after he should have secured a strong place for his government "among the mountains." He therefore built a strong city upon the frontier of his dominions, and called it after his son Beeja, so that it is now known by the name of Beejanuggur. He then raised an army, and put part of it under Krishn Naik, who reduced Wurungul, and compelled Imad-ool-Moolk, the governor, to retreat to Dowlutabad. Bilál Deo and Krishn Naik united their forces with the troops of the Rajahs of Maabú (Malabar) and Dwara Samoodra (the Billals), and expelled the Mahomedan garrisons and posts, "so that within a few months Mahomed Toghluk had no "possession in that quarter of the Deccan except Dowlutabad."

BUKKA AND HARIHARA.

BUKKA and Harihara may therefore have been either fugitives from Wurungul, or may, as Mr. Wilson observes, have been "descended from a series of petty princes or landholders, possibly "feudatories of the Bellál kings, or of 'Pratapa Rudra,' who took advantage of public commotion to "lay the foundation of a new state." Whatever their previous origin was, however, there is no doubt that Bukka and Harihara were the real founders of the Vijya Nuggur, or Beejanuggur monarchy: and from them (Bukka having reigned from A.D. 1334 to 1367, and Harihara from A.D. 1367 to 1391), the genealogy continues unbroken and authenticated, not only by the Mahomedan historians, but from the inscriptions which belong to the Ravenshaw and Mackenzie collections.

The situation of Beejanuggur was admirably selected both as to the defence of the frontier line of the Tumboodra, and as a position from whence all southern and western conquests could be maintained. As part of "Kishkinda," under the name of Humpee, it was ancient sacred and classic ground, being the locality in which some of the heroes of the Mahábharat had slain the Rajah "Wallee," and was already a place of resort and pilgrimage for Hindoos of the Deccan and Canarese provinces. The city,* which included Humpee, was founded on the right, or southern bank of the Tumboodra river, in a plain partly open to the east and west; but to the north-east, bounded by a wild and fantastic group of rocks and hills intermingled, through which only a few passes practicable for footmen existed; and to the north, on the left bank of the river, by a natural outwork of the same description of granite rocks and hills rising to a considerable height, the northern faces of which are almost inaccessible, and which left only a confined space between them and the river. In this small plain was founded the town or suburb of "Anagoondy" (the elephant corner): and what passes there were, being fortified by curtains and bastions, the whole became an almost impregnable position. On the south, the spurs of the lofty Ramandroog hills reached to the city walls, and bounded them on that side; and to the west, the open plain was intersected by fortifications which joined the river on the north bank, and the Ramandroog hills on the south. The enceinte covered a space hardly less than ten square miles, perhaps more, for, including the outwork of Anagoondy, it was not less than four miles in length, by three, or three and a-half, miles in breadth. Between Anagoondy and the city, the river Tumboodra rushes through a gorge of the rocky hills before mentioned—its breadth at one narrow pass being not more than twenty yards—in a series of rapids, which, when the river is in flood, and indeed, at all times, are eminently beautiful; and the scenery, especially if the visitor ascends the river in a basket boat from Anagoondy, to Humpee the ancient and sacred city situated in the gorge already noticed, is throughout most interesting and picturesque. Nowhere in India, or in the world perhaps, have denuded granite rocks, piled upon

* Vide map, page 65.

one another to a height of five or six hundred feet, assumed wilder or more striking forms. In some places, not a shrub occurs to break these marvellously heaped-up masses; in others, they are interspersed by foliage and creepers which hang from them, and soften the effect of their rugged grandeur; and the constantly varying outlines of the rocks and hills, the gloomy effect of the superincumbent masses as the gorge is reached from the long, deep pool below it, the ancient ruined temples on the banks, and the prevailing utter desolation, combine to render an approach to Beejanuggur by the river one of profound interest. The pool below the gorge, from whence the best view of it is obtained, gives as its greatest depth ninety-three feet; and in other parts from sixty to seventy were found by the author of this memoir. The river as is shown by the water-marks in the gorge, rises forty to fifty feet above its ordinary level when in flood, and on these occasions, the turmoil of waters and the vast whirlpools in the reach below, are represented to be sublime.

In this peculiar and interesting locality, therefore, the hereafter famous Hindoo capital of the Beejanuggur dynasty was established, and must have risen very rapidly to eminence. By what means, or at what period the family conquered in succession the provinces to the south and west, can only be conjectured; nor is any record of their early progress existent, except what is supplied by the chronicle of the Bahmuny, Adil Shahy, and Golcondah kings by Ferishta. By Alla-oo-Deen Gungoo Bahmuny, the founder of the first independent Mahomedan dynasty of the Deccan, A. D. 1347, the Beejanuggur princes do not appear to have been molested; but in the reign of his son and successor, Mahomed Shah Bahmuny I, some remarkable events occurred which prove that in A. D. 1368, thirty-four years after its presumed origin, the Beejanuggur kingdom had attained very considerable local power. It was in this year that the Mahomedan king, in the midst of a festival held to celebrate victories over the Hindoo princes of Telingana, gave an order on the treasury of Beejanuggur for the payment of some musicians, which they were to deliver: an insolent act of aggression, which occasioned a memorable and destructive war.

DEVA RAYA.

IT is somewhat difficult to decide who the reigning prince at Beejanuggur was at this precise period. By the Mackenzie inscriptions, Bukka had reigned only five years, 1370-1375; but if his accession, according to Mahdava Acharya's chronicle, be considered as established in 1334, he had reigned forty-one years, an unusually long period; and if, according to the table of inscriptions, Harihara his brother had succeeded him between 1375 and 1385, and reigned till 1429, another extraordinarily long reign must have occurred, and Harihara was alive ninety-five years after the foundation of the city. This is not likely to be the case, and the name of the reigning prince given in the Ravenshaw pedigree is more likely to be the correct one. According to this, therefore, Harihara had died the year before, that is, 1367, or thirty-three years after the foundation of the city, and his son, Deva Raya, or Deo Rai, according to the genealogy, and Krishn Rai, according to Ferishta, could little brook the insult offered by the Mahomedan king. The messenger from Goolburgah was paraded through the city on an ass, and dismissed with insult: and the Rajah, assembling his army, marched with 30,000 horse, 3000 elephants, and 100,000 foot, to Adoni, whence he began to ravage the Mahomedan territory. Among other operations the fort of Moodgul, then held by a Mahomedan garrison, was besieged and taken, and the garrison put to the sword; and news of this event reaching the Mahomedan king, he swore a memorable oath, that "he would not sheathe his sword till he had put to death 100,000 infidels." The Beejanuggur prince must have advanced from Moodgul to the bank of the Krishna, then full, in order to dispute its passage; but this did not deter Mahmood, who crossed the river with 9000 horse, attacked the Hindoos when heavy rain was falling, and, their elephants being unable to act, the rest of the army was seized with a panic, and fled to Adoni, leaving their camp equipage and *guns* in the hands of the enemy. On this occasion Mahmood fell upon the vast Bazaar of camp followers, and slew 70,000 of them; and, making every allowance for exaggeration, it is evident that this was a very bloody defeat. It is especially mentioned that artillery had never heretofore been made use of by Mahomedans in the Deccan; but that captured on this occasion was made over to the command of Sufdur Khan, "to whom was attached a number of Turks and *Europeans* acquainted with the art of gunnery." Following up this victory, Mahmood crossed the Tumboodra, and was met by the army of Beejanuggur, under Bhoj Rai, the Beejanuggur minister, who had vaunted he would bring back the head of the Mahomedan king on a spear. The entire Mahomedan army is described as composed of 15,000 cavalry and 50,000 infantry, of which 10,000 cavalry and 30,000 foot, with the *artillery*, advanced under the King's general, Khan Mahomed, and were met by Bhoj Mul at the head of 40,000 horse and 500,000 foot. There is no doubt that the Mahomedan historian exaggerates the Hindoo host: nevertheless, their army must have been at least equal to the Mahomedan. Each party was inflamed by religious animosity, and the combat was fierce and bloody. The commanders of both wings of the Mahomedans were killed, and their troops broke; when the king, at the head of 3,000 horse, changed the fate of the battle. The artillery, too, had effect upon the Hindoo army, and after a spirited charge by an officer named Mokurrib Khan, in which an elephant became unruly, and, rushing forward, broke the Hindoo line, the day could not be retrieved. Bhoj Mul was killed, and a prodigious slaughter ensued, not only of fighting men, but of the people generally. Krishn Rai fled from place to place, and at last threw himself into the capital, which Mahmood invested; but being unable to make any impression on the fortifications,—it was naturally impregnable at every other point,—the king had recourse to stratagem. He pretended to be ill, and retreated across the Tumboodra, followed by the Hindoos. When the wide plain north of the river had been reached, the king encamped, as did also Krishn Rai. At night Mahmood assembled his principal officers, and opened to them his plan of a night attack on the enemy, which was forthwith put in execution. Krishn Rai and his nobles had passed a night of carousal, and, wearied by it, had gone to sleep; before dawn, however, their camp was furiously attacked by the Mahomedans, and a complete rout ensued, the Rajah saving himself with difficulty. The scene of this event is the plain to the north of the present Gungawutti, and its memory is preserved in local legend at Anagoondi. Mahmood now recrossed the river, and began to massacre the inhabitants of all the villages near the capital. Terror-stricken, the people implored their Rajah to make terms with the fierce Mahomedans; and some of Mahmood's officers are said to have reminded him that his vow of slaughter extended to *only* 100,000 infidels: but though he admitted the sanctity of his vow, the king would be satisfied with nothing short of the payment of his musicians, and the ambassadors from Beejanuggur forthwith paid the amount. "Praise be to God," exclaimed the king, "that what I ordered has been performed; I would not let a light word be recorded of me in the pages of history!" Struck with the remonstrances of the Hindoo ambassadors, the king bound himself by an oath, that henceforward he and his successors would spare all unarmed people in war,—a promise which he at least faithfully observed; and during his reign, which ended by his death in A.D. 1375, no further war with Beejanuggur ensued.

No sooner, however, was his son Mujahid Shah Bahmuny established on the throne, than he sent a demand to Krishn Rai to forego his claims to the territory west of the Tumboodra, to give up the fort of Bunkapoor, and the Dooab between the Krishna and Tumboodra rivers. This arrogant request, as may be supposed, was not complied with; Krishn Rai, on his part, asserted his right to the Dooab, and desired "the elephants taken by King Mahmood might be returned." War, therefore, ensued; the Beejanuggur territory was invaded, and Rajah Krishn Rai, not trusting to the defences of his capital, moved to the westward into the forests and jungles of the ghauts, followed by the king, who penetrated to the sea-coast, and repaired a mosque which had been erected at Seeta Bund Rameshwur by Mullik Kafoor. Krishn Rai had hoped that the climate of the forests would be fatal to the Mahomedans; but it proved unfavourable to himself and his family, and he returned to Beejanuggur. He was pursued by the king, who suddenly appeared in the suburbs of the city, and caused the greatest consternation. The place attacked was, in fact, Cumlapoor, where there was then, and is now, a lake or tank, and a very rich temple upon a rising ground. This temple the king razed to the ground, possessing himself of its jewels, and the gold plates with which the shrine and its pinnacle were covered. Krishn Rai attempted to save it, but failed; his sortie being driven back. During the skirmish the king, with an armour-bearer named Mahmood, went unnoticed to observe the enemy's progress, and was seen by a Hindoo, who immediately attacked him. The armour-bearer's horse rearing, threw him, when the king encountered his adversary in single combat. A blow aimed at his head might have proved fatal, but for the steel casque he wore, and in turn the Hindoo was cloven "from the shoulder to the navel" by the king, who was remarkable for his personal strength, and fell dead from his horse. Mujahid Shah then assisted his servant to remount, and they rode back amidst the acclamations of both armies, "the Hindoos being unable to restrain their admiration of such gallantry." A general action followed, which appears, from Ferishta's interesting and graphic account of it, to have been fought with great valour and much military skill on each side. Mokurrib Khan, the commander of the artillery, was killed, with many others. Mujahid Shah was in every part of the field by turns, slaying numbers with his own hand. The key of the position was an eminence named Dhuna Sódra, where Mujahid Shah had posted his uncle, Dawood Khan. This officer, however, considering that the royal army required reinforcement, left the hill with his force and mingled in the fray, having three horses killed under him. It may be gathered from the chronicle, that although the Mahomedans claimed a victory, they were nevertheless obliged to retreat. The Dhuna Sodra position would have covered this manœuvre, and had evidently been taken up for the purpose; and the king moved a large force to retake it, when it was abandoned by the Hindoos, and reoccupied by the king in person, who remained there till the last of his army had passed the defile. No further attack of Beejanuggur followed, and the king, with between sixty and seventy thousand captives, moved towards Adoni.

Ferishta's enumeration of the size of the kingdom of Beejanuggur at this period supplies a hiatus which no inscriptions or other records afford. He describes it as extending from the Krishna to Rameshwur, "and from the "shores of the Indian ocean to Telingana." It is questionable whether the actual administrative authority of the State ever reached as far as the extreme southern point of the peninsula; but the Beejanuggur princes may even then have been powerful enough to levy tribute from the Pandyan kings of Madura and the Cholas of Conjeveram (Kunchi), both of which kingdoms were declining. They were certainly more important than the Mahomedans in the time of Mujahid Shah, who, as Ferishta observes, only maintained their superiority by their valour; and in wealth and extent of country the Rajahs of Beejanuggur greatly exceeded them. The port of Goa, the fortress of Belgaum, and many other places to the westward of Beejanuggur, with the Konkan, belonged to the Hindoo kingdom; and the rulers of Malabar, Ceylon, and other countries, kept ambassadors at the court. "The ancestors of Krishn Rai," writes Ferishta, "had possessed this kingdom for 'seven hundred years,' during "which period, being undisturbed by revolution and sparing in expense, their treasures had so accumulated as "to equal those of all the kings of the earth; and in the time of Alla-oo-Deen Khiljy, the grandfather of "Krishn Rai had buried part of his treasures, which fell into the hands of some of the chiefs of Alla-oo-Deen, "at Seeta Bund Raméshwur where they had been concealed."

By this account, Ferishta would give a much more ancient origin to the kingdom than may be inferred from the table of inscriptions; and, though vaguely, confirms the genealogical period embraced in Mr. E. C. Ravenshaw's list, which was supplied by the hereditary Guru, or chief priest, of the family, and also the history of Mahdáva Achárya. At the same time, it is strange that no mention of such a kingdom is found in the record of Mullik Kafoor's expedition to Dwára Samoodra, when, if there had existed a rich city like Beejanuggur, it would unquestionably have been plundered and its dynasty destroyed, as that of the Bellâls was at Dwára Samoodra. The rise of the Mahomedan power in the Deccan, from the first invasion in 1294 to its greatness displayed in the condition of the Bahmuny kingdom in 1378, a period of eighty-four years, might easily be equalled, if not, indeed, surpassed, by an active Hindoo power which, of the same faith as the conquered people, and fully acquainted with their social condition, would have less trouble in establishing their government than Mahomedans, necessarily ignorant on all points, both of character and language. It is very probable, too, that the fortifications of Beejanuggur, which consisted of several lines, were extended only as required; and the original may not have been larger than the citadel itself; nay, that the successive Mahomedan attacks of the suburbs may have led, as was the case at Beejapoor, to the outworks being extended to a distance of many miles. Notwithstanding Ferishta's account of the age of the dynasty, confirmed by Mr. Ravenshaw's genealogy, the real date of the rise of Beejanuggur, under the brothers Bukka and Harihara, does not seem to be materially affected, and the dates of the inscriptions are in the main confirmed.

Déva Rai, or, according to the Mahomedan orthography, Déo Rai, reigned from A.D. 1391 to 1414; and in the year 1398, peace having subsisted between the rival kingdoms for twenty years, war again broke out between them. On this occasion, Déva Rai, according to Ferishta, was the aggressor, having suddenly invaded the Koolburgah territory (Feroze Shah Bahmuny being king) with 30,000 horse and a vast army of foot, his object being to possess himself of the Rachore Dooab, and the forts of Rachore and Moodgul. He was met by king Feroze on the banks of the Krishna; but his son having been assassinated by an emissary of the king, Déva Rai fled precipitately, and shut himself up in Beejanuggur. He was followed by the Mahomedans, who again laid waste the country south of that city, and their forbearance was only purchased by the payment of eleven lacs of hoons (about £450,000), the Mahomedans retaining possession of the disputed territory. This peace did not, however, continue, for in A.D. 1406, the Rajah having heard of the beautiful daughter of a goldsmith who resided at Moodgul, sent a detachment of his troops to carry her off; but the girl had fled with her parents, and the troops, in revenge for their disappointment, ravaged the country on their return. Feroze Shah was by no means a character to be insulted with impunity, and forthwith marched upon Beejanuggur, and in the first assault obtained a footing in the place; but this could not be maintained, and the Mahomedan army, taking up a position without, remained there for several months, the time being occupied by continual skirmishes. A portion of King Feroze's forces were however, sent once more to ravage the southern provinces of Beejanuggur, and by another detachment the fort of Bunkapoor was besieged and taken. Déva Rai had failed in obtaining assistance from the kings of Malwa, Khandésh, and Guzerat, and alarmed at King Feroze's intention of attacking Adoni, sued for peace. On this occasion the king would be content with nothing short of Déva Rai's daughter in marriage, with a portion of ten lacs of hoons (£400,000), five muns (120lbs. weight) of pearls, fifty elephants, and two thousand slaves, together with the fort and dependencies of Bunkapoor. Déva Rai hesitated for a time; but was eventually obliged to accede to these terms, and to give his daughter in marriage to the king. This wedding was forthwith celebrated with great pomp, and animosities for the time were suspended; but King Feroze conceived himself affronted by a breach of Mahomedan etiquette, and the marriage does not appear to have led to any cordiality on either side. No fresh war occurred, however, till after the accession of Ahmed Shah Wully Bahmuny, the brother of Feroze, who succeeded him; and in the first year of his reign (1422-23) the territories of Beejanuggur were again invaded.

By this time, according to Mr. Ravenshaw's genealogy, Déva Rai had been succeeded by Vijaya Rai in 1414; and if this account of reigning princes be correct, it was with him that the war occurred. Mr. Wilson's list of inscriptions, however, gives dates of grants by Déva Raya as late as 1458, and the complications increase, if the lists quoted by Mr. H. H. Wilson, and Colonel Mackenzie, &c. are compared with the others; in fact the whole become irreconcileable one with another, both as to names and dates. For this reason, and because it may be necessary to refer to each, they will be given separately at the conclusion of this memoir. In regard to the present quarrel, however, there seems no doubt that the tribute payable under the first treaty, and the enforcement of its liquidation, was the ostensible object of the Mahomedan expedition. In this respect the Mahomedan king was successful. Beejanuggur was again closely besieged, and the tribute eventually sent to the royal camp with all requisite honours, the Rajah's son accompanying it, and escorting the Koolburgah monarch to the frontier. After this, mutual engagements seem to have been observed for some years, and no further cause of dispute is mentioned; but on the accession of Alla-oo-Deen Bahmuny II. in 1435, an arrear of tribute of five years was due, and the king's brother, Prince Mahomed Khan, was sent with an army to demand it. At the head of this army, and in possession of the tribute money which had been paid—instigated moreover by some of the commanders of the royal troops—the prince rebelled against his brother; and being assisted by the Rajah of Beejanuggur, occupied the districts of Beejapoor, Sholapoor, and Nuldroog in succession, in addition to the Rachore Dooab. Vijaya Rai, who had succeeded Déva Raya in A.D. 1414 (if Mr. Ravenshaw's list be correct), had reigned till 1424, when he was followed by Pundára Déva Rai. It was this prince therefore, who, under the appellation of Déo Rai, Ferishta accuses of having abetted the Prince Mahomed Khan's design of dividing the Bahmuny kingdom. The enterprise however failed, for in a general action the prince and his partisans were defeated; and it is interesting to observe that King Alla-oo-Deen not only forgave his brother, but settled Rachore upon him, where he lived many years.

The galling, and always successfully enforced, payment of tribute to the Bahmuny kings, due under the first treaty with Mahmood Shah Bahmuny I, was unendurable by Pandára Déo Rai; and he began to consider that a conquest of the whole of the Bahmuny territories might be practicable. Now also, for the first time, he enlisted Mahomedans in his army, and built a mosque for them in his capital, allowing them free exercise of their faith. He also introduced archery into his own army, and 60,000 of his troops were instructed in the art. Finally, in 1443, he crossed the Tumboodra and overran the Dooab, his light troops plundering the country as far as Sugger and Beejapoor. An interesting confirmation of this war occurs in the journal of Abd-ul-Ruzzák, a Mahomedan gentleman, who was sent from Mirza Shah Rókh, King of Khorassán, as ambassador to India in 1442-3. The exact object of the embassy does not transpire; but the descriptions of the ambassador's residence at Beejanuggur, of the capital, and of local occurrences, are in the highest degree interesting, not only as pictures of the time—drawn with very evident truth—but as the only ones existent. "At "this period (1443)," writes the ambassador, "Daiang, the vizier, who manifested to the author of this work "the most lively interest, set out on an expedition into the kingdom of Kulbergah. The reasons which "led to this invasion are as follows:—The King of Kulbergah, Alla-ed-din Ahmed Schah, having heard "of the conspiracy formed against the life of Diou-rai (Déva Rai), and of the assassination of the principal "persons attached to the government of this prince, had received the intelligence with extreme delight. He "sent to this monarch an eloquent messenger charged with the following message:—'Send me a sum of seven "'lacs of "Varahas" (hoons), or else I will march into your country a formidable army, and I will overturn, "'from its foundation, the empire of idolatry.' Diou Rai, the king of Bidganugger, was equally troubled and "irritated by the receipt of such a message. On receiving it he said, 'Since I am alive, what cause of alarm "'can there be because certain of my servants are killed? If my enemies flatter themselves that they will find "'in me weakness, negligence, idleness, or apathy, it goes for nothing. I am protected by a powerful and "'happy star; Fortune watches over me with affection. Meanwhile, whatever my enemies may find "'themselves able to take from my kingdom will be in their eyes a booty for them to distribute among their "'"Seids" and their learned men. Whereas, for my part, whatever shall fall into my power out of the "'territories of my enemies shall be given by me to the *bázdárs* (falconers) and to the Brahmins.' Troops "were sent out on both sides, which made great ravages on the frontiers of the two kingdoms." From the foregoing account, which has every mark of perfect correctness, the inference arises that the seven lacs of hoons demanded were probably an arrear of tribute, and that the refusal of payment led to the war. In all other respects, as to date, the names of the kings, Alla-oo-Deen and Diou Raia, (Déva Rai), the confirmation is very exact. It is impossible, however, to leave this interesting journal without noticing its contents in other respects.

Abd-ul-Ruzzák left Persia in January 1442; and after visiting Ormuz and other maritime cities, arrived at length at Calicut in the beginning of 1443. His sufferings from sea-sickness, his dislike of that town, his descriptions of the almost naked "Zamori," of his equally naked court, and his own various annoyances—are graphically and very amusingly described. Calicut is mentioned as a thriving seaport, whence vessels sail constantly for "Mecca," laden with pepper; and the sailors are especially brave and venturous. The Zamori, though not a subject of the King of Beejanuggur, yet pays him respect, and is extremely in fear of him. During his stay at Calicut, a messenger from "Bidganugger" arrives with a letter, to be forwarded to the ambassador of the Persian king, and Abd-ul-Ruzzák determines to proceed thither. He accordingly goes by sea to Mangalore, which forms the frontier of the "Bidganugger" kingdom. It is evident, therefore, that the conquests of the Beejanuggur State had extended very considerably to the south, and at this period probably comprised the whole of Mysore. At Mangalore and Beyloor the Hindoo temples are described to be magnificent, and seem to have struck the traveller with great amazement; and finally he reaches the city of "Bidganugger" about the end of April 1443, is favourably received, and a handsome house allotted to him for residence. "The city is large," he writes, "and thickly peopled; and the king possesses sovereignty in the "highest degree, his dominions extending from the extremity of the country of Kulbergah to Serendib (Ceylon). "It is for the most part well cultivated, very fertile, and contains more than three hundred harbours. One "sees there more than a thousand elephants, and the troops amount in number to eleven lac (1,100,000). "One might seek in vain throughout the whole of Hindoostan to find a more absolute Rái (king)." The city is then described, and compared with Herat. First, the citadel; then, the second fortress, and the third, fourth, fifth, and sixth enclosures. The seventh contains the palace of the king, and is near the centre of all. The distance from the gate of the first fortress, which lies on the north "Anagoondi," to the first gate which is situated in the south, is calculated to be two parasangs, and it is the same distance from east to west. The space which separates the first fortress from the second, and up to the third fortress, is filled with cultivated fields, and with houses and gardens. At the gate of the king's palace are four bazaars placed opposite to each other.

"Above each bazaar is a lofty areade, with a magnificent gallery; but the audience hall of the king's palace is "elevated above all the rest. The bazaars are extremely long and broad. The rose merchants place before "their shops high *estradas*, on each side of which they expose their flowers for sale. In this place one sees "a succession of sweet-smelling and fresh-looking roses; the people could not live without them, and con- "sider them quite as necessary as food. Each class of men belonging to each profession has shops contiguous "one to the other. The jewellers sell publicly in the bazaar rubies, emeralds, diamonds, and pearls. In this "agreeable locality, as well as in the king's palace, are numerous running streams and canals, formed of "chiselled stone, polished and smooth. On the left of the Sultan's palace, rises the Divàn Khaneh (council "house), which is extremely large, and looks like a palace. Here the scribes sit, and their writing is of two "kinds. In one they write with a Kalam (style) of iron, upon a leaf of the Indian nut tree, which is two "ghez " (a ghez is about three-quarters of a yard) in length, and two fingers in breadth. These characters "have no colour, and the writing lasts but a short time. In the second kind of writing, they blacken a white "surface; they then take a soft stone (potstone), which they cut like a kalam, and use to form the letters; "this stone leaves on the black surface a white colour, which lasts a long time, and this kind of writing is held "in high estimation." The ambassador would appear, however, to have confounded the two processes, that graven on the leaf by the iron style, and still used, being permanent, and the other perishable. Money is coined in the royal mint, both gold and silver, as well as copper; and the soldiers receive their pay every four months direct from the treasury, no orders being given on the provinces. All the inhabitants of the country, both those of exalted rank and of inferior classes, down to the very artisans, wear pearls, or rings adorned with precious stones, in their ears, on their necks, on their arms, on the upper part of the head, and on the fingers.

It was on the 1st of May, 1443, that Abd-ul-Ruzzák took up his abode in the city, and rested several days; but he was speedily sent for to court, and offered five beautiful horses and some "tokouz" of damask and satin. The prince was seated in a hall surrounded by the most imposing attributes of state. Right and left of him stood a numerous crowd of men ranged in a circle. The king was dressed in a robe of green satin; around his neck he wore a collar of pearls of beautiful water, and other splendid gems. He had an olive complexion, his frame was thin, and he was rather tall. On his cheeks might be seen a slight down, but there was no beard on his chin. The expression of his countenance was extremely pleasing. "The monarch received me with "interest, and made me take a seat very near him." The Persian king's letter was then presented, and graciously received, and the Rajah, observing that Abd-ul-Ruzzák was, as he describes, "showered in "perspiration, owing to the number of robes he wore, sent him a fan." He was then courteously dismissed with betel and a purse of gold placed upon a salver, and a daily allowance of "two sheep, four pairs "of fowls, five mun of rice, one of butter, one of sugar, and two 'Varahas' of gold," and the Rajah sent the following message:—"Your monarchs invite an ambassador, and receive him at their table; as you and we "may not eat together, this purse full of gold is the feast we give to an ambassador." Abd-ul-Ruzzak is accused, however, of not being an ambassador at all, but only a travelling merchant, and his allowance of food and money is stopped. Daiang, the vizier, is absent in the Kulburgah war, and a Christian named Nimeh, or Mineh-pezir, has taken his place in the royal council, and evinces anything but a friendly spirit. "Daiang," however, returns after a while, and Abd-ul-Ruzzák receives 7000 váráhás in gold from the royal treasury (about 1200*l*.), perhaps the price of his horses and merchandize, and his dismissal, and seems glad to get away from Beejanuggur, although the Rajah assured him of honourable reception if he returned properly accredited. It is impossible to give more than a mere sketch of this clever journal, else interesting extracts might be made from the author's account of the festival of Mahnadi, probably the Dussera, or Mahnúmi, which he witnessed. Then, "in pursuance of orders issued by the King of Beejanuggur, the generals and principal "personages from all parts of his empire, which extended over a space of three months' journey, presented "themselves at the palace. They brought with them a thousand elephants, resembling the waves of a troubled "sea, or a stormy cloud, which were covered with brilliant armour, and with castles magnificently adorned, in "which were jugglers and artificers; on the trunks and ears of these animals had been drawn with cinnabar and "other substances extraordinary pictures, and figures of wonderful beauty. The vast space of land "magnificently decorated, in which the enormous elephants are congregated together, presented the appearance "of the waves of the sea, or of that compact mass of men which will be assembled together at the day of "resurrection." On this magnificent space were erected numerous pavilions, to the height of three, four, and five stories, covered from top to bottom with figures in relief, everything, down to flies and gnats, being drawn with extraordinary skill and delicacy. Some of these pavilions were so arranged that they could turn round rapidly and present a new face. In front of all rose the king's palace of nine pavilions, magnificently ornamented; before this the athletic games, the juggling tricks, the plays, orations, recitations, and dancing, continued uninterruptedly from morning to night for three days. Abd-ul-Ruzzák's descriptions of these royal festivities are curiously correct and unexaggerated; and indeed in all other respects his journal throws a valuable light upon the condition of Beejanuggur at the period of his visit, and shows also how little the native manners, customs, and festivals, have changed up to the present time.

Abd-ul-Ruzzák especially mentions that the King or Rajah of Beejanuggur did not go in person to the war while he was at the capital; but it is by no means improbable that he did not take the field after the magnificent Dussera, or "Mahnadi" festival described, which, there can be little doubt, was the assembling of troops for the campaign. Ferishta records that the Bahmuny king met the Hindoos on the old ground near Moodgul, and that in two months there were three great actions. Moodgul, at this period, was held by the Hindoos; and after one of the engagements, two officers of the Kulburgah army, having chased the flying Hindoos into the fort, were taken prisoner, whereupon the Bahmuny king wrote to the Rajah that he valued these officers' lives at a hundred thousand Hindoos each, and that he would slay that number for each if their lives were sacrificed. Such grim threats of the Bahmuny princes were never without signification; and the officers were not only released, but peace ensued, the Rajah paying up arrears of tribute and presenting forty elephants, receiving in return valuable presents. Nor did any fresh cause of war occur up to the period of Alla-oo-Deen Bahmuny's death in 1455.

Ramchundra Rai had succeeded Pundara Deva Rai in 1450, and reigned till 1473. Alla-oo-Deen Bahmuny had been succeeded by Hoomayoon the Cruel in 1455; he, by Nizam Shah in 1461; and he in turn by Mahomed II. in 1463, who reigned till 1482, and was followed by Mahmood Shah II, the last king who preserved any semblance of authority in the once powerful Bahmuny kingdom. From the period of the war with Alla-oo-Deen Bahmuny, therefore, in 1442-3, up to the declaration of independence, in 1489, by Yoosuf Adil Shah, of Beejapoor, a period of forty-six years, no disagreement appears to have occurred between the Mahomedans and the Hindoos of Beejanuggur; nor were the Mahomedans, on account of internal dissensions, mutual jealousies, and the rapidly advancing dismemberment of the Bahmuny kingdom, in a condition to have waged war with the united and powerful state of Beejanuggur.

The absence of any historical record of domestic occurrences at Beejanuggur, such as was maintained at all the Mahomedan courts of India, prevents the possibility of discovering the progress the Hindoo kingdom had made from 1442 to 1490. Nor do the details of the Beejanuggur inscriptions, beyond mention of the names of the princes by whom, or in whose reigns, they were made, give any clue to the progress of public events. To Ramchundra Rai succeeded Narsinha Rajah in A.D. 1473, and Vira, or Veer Narsinha Rajah in 1490 (the last being authenticated by inscriptions), who had three sons, Achút, Sadashew, and Trimala. These being minors, the country was managed by Krishn Rai, their father's brother, who had previously held the office of prime minister. The inscription list confirms the three names, but makes them princes reigning as follows:—

Achútya, from 1530 to 1542;
Sadasiva from 1542 to 1570;
Trimala, from 1568 to 1571.

This period is nearly identical with the declaration of independence by Yoosuf Adil Shah at Beejapoor; but it is improbable, perhaps, that any disagreement would have occurred between him and the Rajah of Beejanuggur, when he was himself struggling into political existence—certain that he would not have provoked war. Kasim Bereed, however, the restless and intriguing minister of the remnant of the Bahmuny kingdom, being unable to oppose the power of Yoosuf Adil Shah, offered the Beejanuggur minister the tempting bribe of the Rachore Dooab, and the forts of Rachore and Moodgul, if he would assist in crushing the newly-formed kingdom of Beejapoor. It was accepted, and an army sent to take possession. Had the confederates against Yoosuf Adil Shah been able to act in concert, it is very probable he could not have retained the territory he had seized; but no simultaneous movement was made. The Beejapoor king entered into a treaty with the Beejanuggur general, and for a time danger from that quarter was averted. Ferishta hints that local quarrels at Beejanuggur between the Regent, whom he calls Timraj, and the young Rajah, prevented for awhile any prosecution of the war; but as soon as these were adjusted, the Beejanuggur army was put in motion against Yoosuf Ádil Shah, and was defeated with immense slaughter in April, 1493; on which occasion the Hindoos lost their treasure and camp equipage, and the young Rajah died, on his way to Beejanuggur, of wounds received in the action. Ferishta's chronicle, in this respect, appears to be confirmed by Mr. Ravenshaw's "Genealogy," for no period is given for Achút Rai's reign, though he is mentioned between Veer Narsimha and Krishn Déva Máha Raja. It therefore appears uncertain whether the Krishn Déva who succeeded in 1524 is the son of Achút Rai, or the uncle and regent, who may have usurped the throne; most probably, however, the latter, and it is evident that in 1530 some domestic revolution had occurred at Beejanuggur, for Ismail Adil Shah marched from Beeder southwards without interruption. "The affairs of the kingdom of Beejanuggur," writes Ferishta, "had lately "been thrown into confusion, owing to the death of Tima Raj, to whom his son, Ram Raj, had succeeded. "Against this prince rebellions were excited by several Ráis, so that the Mahomedans met with no interruption "to their progress, and Rachore and Moodgul both surrendered by capitulation, after having been in possession "of the 'infidels' for seventeen years."

By the "Genealogy," however, Krishn Deva Maha Raya ascended the throne in 1524: and at this time the Hindoo kingdom had perhaps attained its greatest eminence and extent. During the long interval of peace with the Mahomedans, the Beejanuggur conquests had been extended to Maha-nád, near Ramnád; Kunchi, and Choldesh, the capital and country of the Cholas; Pandu Desh, or Madura; Sriranga, or Seringapatam; Arcot, Nellore, Mysore, Ahmednagur (?), Soonda, Chittledroog, Hurpunhullee, Kurpah (Cuddapa), Yadagéri (Yadgeer), Rachore, Gudwall, Kurnool, Shorapoor, Sugger, and many others. It is evident that those places mentioned to the north of the Krishna, that is, Kulburgah, Ahmednuggur, Guzerat, &c, are mere vaunts, since Mahomedan dynasties were then reigning there; but it seems very possible that the whole of the south had been overrun: that the actual dominions of Beejanuggur reached to the southern border of the plateau of Mysore, and that the remnants of the Pandu and Chola kingdoms acknowledged its power and paid it tribute. Mr. H. H. Wilson, on the authority of a local chronicle, states that Krishn Raya was the illegitimate son of Raja Narsimha, a prince of Telinga extraction, by whom the ancient line was supplanted in the latter end of the fifteenth century. It had been impossible for him to remain at court; but on his death-bed, his father's affliction at his absence induced the minister to summon the young prince, who was declared successor to the throne, to the exclusion of his elder and legitimate brother. This chronicle also gives testimony to the vigour and ability of Krishn Raya. He was the only Beejanuggur prince who ever obtained advantages over the Mahomedans; and he invaded Orissa, the daughter of whose king he married, and extended the authority, if not the actual conquests, of Beejanuggur, over the whole of the south of India. The domestic quarrel at Beejanuggur was most probably between Krishn Rai, who had usurped the throne, and Rama Rajah, who deposed and succeeded him. The names, at least, agree with those of the Mahomedan history, which, from the details that Ferishta gives, is most likely to be the true one. By his account, when a Rajah who is named "Shew Rai," (possibly Veer Narsinha), or, as it is locally pronounced, "Narshew," died, he was succeeded by his son, a minor, who did not long survive him, and left the throne to a younger brother. Not long after, he died also, leaving an infant only three months old. Timraj became regent, and on the king's attaining manhood, he was poisoned. This was, perhaps, Achút Rai. Another infant (possibly Sadasiva) was put on the throne, Timraj retaining his regency. Timraj is succeeded by his brother-in-law, Ramraj, in regard to whose name both authorities agree. "Ramraj," says the chronicle, "in "the course of five or six years had cut off by treachery all who opposed his pretensions to the throne." And this seems to have been a matter of universal notoriety. Believing himself secure, he left the city in charge of a dependant, and went southwards to punish some rebellious feudatories, when a reaction arose in favour of the ancient family; and the uncle of the infant prince, Bhoj Trimala, assembled troops and defied the regent, who submitted to what could not be avoided. Shortly afterwards, Bhoj Trimala Rai, having himself strangled the child, usurped the throne; but being nearly an idiot, and a tyrant to boot, the people became impatient of him, and invited back Ramraj. At this crisis, Bhoj Trimala offered a large subsidy to Ibrahim Adil Shah I. for his support, and the Mahomedan king repaired to Beejanuggur, where he was royally entertained, and Bhoj Trimala duly established on the throne. The introduction of a Mahomedan power, however, into the local politics of Beejanuggur, was by no means acceptable to the nobility and the Brahmin priesthood. As soon as Ibrahim Adil Shah had been paid and dismissed, a revolution in favour of Ramraj occurred, and, on pretence of avenging the death of the infant whom Bhoj Raj had strangled, that person was attacked. Finding he had no chance of success, and indeed under every symptom of insanity, Bhoj Raj destroyed himself by falling upon his sword, after he had ground all the royal jewels to powder, cut off the tails of the elephants and horses, and blinded them. Henceforth Ramraj ruled supreme in reality, but ostensibly as the minister of the sons of Krishn Ráya, Achútya, Trimala, and Sadasiva in succession.

Ibrahim Adil Shah I. died in 1557, and was succeeded by his son Ali. At first Ali Adil Shah courted alliance with Ramraj, and even on one occasion went to visit him in person. These civilities led to a treaty of offensive and defensive alliance against the state of Ahmednuggur, then very powerful; and a letter written by Ramraj to Ibrahim Kootub Shah, King of Golcondah, who had espoused the other side, while it explains the political position of all parties, will serve as a specimen of the intelligent and courteous style of diplomatic intercourse then existent among native princes of India. "Be it known unto your majesty," writes Ramraj, "that it is now many "years since the courts of Beejapoor and Ahmednuggur have been in a constant state of warfare, and that the "balance of power between them was so equal, that although every year each of these sovereigns had been in the "habit of making a campaign on each other's frontiers, yet no advantage occurred to either. It now appears "that your majesty (whose ancestors never appeared in these disputes) has marched an army to turn the scale in "favour of Hussein Nizam Shah, without having any cause of enmity against Ibrahim Adil Shah of Beejapoor, "who has accordingly sought our alliance. As a friendship has long subsisted between our court and your majesty, "we have thought fit to lay these arguments before you, to induce you to relinquish the offensive alliance which "your majesty has formed, and by returning peaceably to your capital show a friendly disposition towards both "parties, who will afterwards conclude a peace, and put an end to this long protracted war." This letter was written at the close of the reign of Ibrahim Adil Shah I, and for a time served its purpose; but on the accession of his son Ali, the Ahmednuggur and Golcondah offensive alliance against Beejapoor was renewed; and the Beejapoor and Beejanuggur kings having coalesced, invaded Ahmednuggur and besieged the capital. During this campaign the Hindoo auxiliaries behaved with such barbarity, that although Ramraj, under the remonstrances of the King of Golcondah, was eventually induced to return to his capital, his overbearing conduct had the effect of causing all the Mahomedan kings of the Deccan to combine in a crusade against him. In the year 1564, the plans of the confederates were matured; and having united their forces, they advanced southwards by way of Talikota. The Beejanuggur troops had taken up the line of the Krishna as their most advantageous position; but the allies crossed by a skilfully managed manœuvre, and a general action ensued at about ten miles south of the river, where the Hindoos had formed their camp. It is almost impossible to come to a correct conclusion of the numbers of the forces engaged on each side in this decisive battle. Ramraj is said to have had 70,000 cavalry and 90,000 foot, archers and matchlock men, in the field; and indeed by other accounts very many more. The Mahomedans, united, were not probably less than 100,000 strong. During the progress of the fight, all accounts concur in stating that both wings of the Mahomedan army had fallen back, and that little more was needed to insure their complete defeat; but the centre was firmly held by the King of Ahmednugger, with his famous artillery, on which the Hindoos could make no impression. He had no less than 100 guns of all descriptions posted in three lines, the heavy pieces in the first, the light artillery in the second, and in the third "zumbooruks," or swivels. Chuleby Roomy Khan, a European Turk, commanded the whole. The line was masked by 2000 archers, who fell back behind the guns when they were charged, and assisted their destructive effect. Ramraj, who commanded the centre of his own army, after the failure of the first charge against the guns which he had directed in person, began to distribute rewards to incite another, which was made. On this occasion the guns were loaded with bags of the heavy copper money of the country, which caused a terrible slaughter. Five thousand Hindoos are said to have fallen at the muzzles of the guns; and Kishwur Khan Lary, at the head of 5000 Beejapoor cavalry, charging through the intervals of the artillery, carried all before him, when the Beejanuggur army was irretrievably routed. Ramraj himself, who was endeavouring to escape on foot, was seized and beheaded, and his army fled to Beejanuggur, where it was pursued by the Mahomedans.

A most interesting confirmation of the events of this war, and of the condition of Beejanuggur, after its plunder by the Mahomedans, occurs in the voyages of M. Cæsar Fredericke, a Venetian merchant, who visited that city in 1565. The great battle had been fought in December 1564, or January 1565; and M. Fredericke was at Beejanuggur for seven months after the Mahomedans had left it, and while one of Ramraj's sons. Timraj, was purchasing horses, and endeavouring to reconstruct the army. M. Fredericke's account of the battle is as follows:—

"The city of Bezeneger was sacked in the year 1565 by four kings of the Moors, who were of great "power and might. The first was called Dialcan (Adil Khan), the second Zamaluc (Nizam-ool-Moolk), the "third Cotamaluc (Kootub-ool-Moolk), and the fourth Viridy (Bereed), and yet these four kings were not "able to overcome this city and the king of Bezeneger but by treason. This king of Bezeneger was a Gentile, "and had amongst all other of his captains two which were notable, and they were Moors; and these "captains had either of them in charge threescore and ten or fourscore thousand men. . . . When the armies "were joined, the battle lasted but for a while, not the space of four hours; because the two traitorous "captains, in the chiefest of the fight, with their companions, turned against their king, and made such disorder "in their army that they set themselves to flight." Some years before, the Rajahs of Beejanuggur had enlisted Mahomedan troops; and Ein-ool-Moolk, who had been previously an officer in the service of the King of Golcondah, is mentioned, in Ferishta's history of that kingdom, as an active partisan of the Beejanuggur state, with the command of 15,000 cavalry, in the year 1563. It is very possible, therefore, that the Mahomedan commanders and their troops may have been corrupted: and there is the more foundation for this belief from the fact that this war was a Jehád, or holy crusade, for the destruction of "infidels." The treachery would serve only, however, to give a different colour to the result of the great battle; for of what followed there is no doubt whatever, as well from Cæsar Fredericke's account as from all other sources. "For "thirty years," he writes, "had three brothers kept their rightful sovereigns in prison. They were "originally servants of a prince who died, leaving an infant son, when they governed in his name. The "chiefest of the three was called Ramaragio (Ramraj), and sat on the royal throne, and was called the "king. The second was called Temiragio (Timraj), and he took the government upon him. The third "was called 'Bengotre' (Venketadri?), and he was captain general of the army. These three were in the "battle, in the which the chiefest (Ramraj), and last (Venketadri), were never heard of quick or dead "Only Temiragio fled in the battle, having lost one of his eyes. When the news came to the city of the "overthrow in the battle, the wives and children of these three tyrants, with their lawful king kept prisoner, "fled away, spoiled as they were; and the four kings of the Moors entered the city of Bezeneger, with great "triumph, and there remained six months, searching under houses and in all places for money and other things "that were hidden; and then they departed to their own kingdom, because they were not able to maintain "such a kingdom as that was, so far distant from their own country."

After their departure Timraj returned, and tried to repopulate the city, but failed. The seat of government was then fixed at Pencondah, a strong hill fort and large town on the borders of Mysore; and here the family remained. Cæsar Fredericke's description of Beejanuggur agrees with that of Abd-ul-Ruzzák, and with its actual condition. "The city," he says, "is not altogether destroyed, yet the houses stand still, but empty; "and there is dwelling in them nothing, as reported, but tigers and other wild beasts. The circuit of the city "is four-and-twenty miles about, and within the walls are several mountains. The houses stand walled with "earth, and are plain, all saving the three palaces of the three tyrant brethren, and the pagodas, which are idol "houses; these are made with lime and fine marble."

Cæsar Fredericke states that the country was in much confusion; "there were many kings, and great "divisions in that kingdom." Every petty chieftain or baron had no doubt asserted his independence. "Every "one of them had stamped new coins, so that the money of one day would not serve the next." And it was with great difficulty that he made his way to the coast through these separate territories. These independent baronies—Hurpunhullee, Chittuldroog, and the like—were held by Beydur chiefs, who had probably owned but light allegiance to Beejanuggur; and they were gradually settled, and their possessions secured to them by Ali Adil Shah, who eventually established his authority over the provinces which lay immediately south and west of Beejanuggur, while the Golcondah kings pressed on southwards in the direction of Pencondah, which afterwards, was sometimes in the hands of one party and sometimes of the other.

Once deserted by its people, the vast city of Beejanuggur must have crumbled away to utter destruction in the course of a very few years. The houses were built of stone and mud, with clay roofs, which require constant repair to keep them stable. One year's neglect would ensure destruction; and whether of one or two stories, the result would be equally certain. All that was built with lime and mortar has survived the lapse of 300 years, and is as perfect as ever. The audience hall of the king's palace, a very elegant building, in the Mahomedan style, the royal elephant-stables, which consist of a long arcade of arches supporting flat-domed ceilings, a beautiful tower, said to have been the place where the infant king was imprisoned, the king's bath, the treasury, the fortifications, the gates, the cut stone channels for water and irrigation, the raised pavement of the principal bazaar, and the terraces on which wares were set out, with the temples, are all still perfect; and a portion of the palace, because of its peculiar roof, more so than any royal dwelling at Beejapoor. It consists of two stories, and is an elegant but curious mixture of Mahomedan with Hindoo architecture. Elsewhere, over the vast enceinte, there is nothing to be seen but continuous mounds of earth and stones, which have been houses and streets, and a few handsome temples; but the principal religious edifices were erected within the precincts of the ancient and sacred city of Humpee, by the river bank, on ground which to all Hindoos was hallowed by the actions and legends of the heroes of the Rámáyun and Mahábhárat.

In addition to the edifices constructed by this remarkable dynasty, some of their admirably useful works of irrigation still remain, and are used now with as good effect as they were at the time of the Mahomedan conquest. At the village of Hoolegee, a few miles above Beejanuggur, the first great weir, or anicut, occurs which supplied the city with water, and irrigated thousands of acres of land on both sides of the river. This weir belongs half to the Nizam, and half to the British Government, and is kept in perfect repair. The weir on the left channel bears an inscription that it was the work of "Achút Rayeel," which was the actual title of the dynasty in A.D. 1535, and as he was a minor, it was probably executed by Krishna Rai, the minister, who afterwards usurped the crown. From Hoolegee to below Kumply, the whole of both banks of the river, wherever water can be led or used, is a beautiful area of rice and sugar-cane cultivation, interspersed with plantations of cocoa-nut trees, which here thrive with great luxuriance. The ground on the right bank belongs to the British Government, that on the left to His Highness the Nizam; among the beautiful villages of which stand the wonderful rocks of Anagoondy, and the town, which is the capital of the small remnant of this once magnificent kingdom. The present Rajah of Anagoondy holds it, and several villages in Jahgeer, from His Highness the Nizam; and the whole supply a revenue of about 20,000 rupees per year (2000*l.*), which, with a nearly similar amount from the British Government, enable the present possessor to live in comfort and respectability.

Little is known of the Beejanuggur family after their removal to Pencondah, where, weakened as they were by the loss of their capital, they had to encounter the forces of the Golcondah king, which were perhaps stronger than those of Beejapoor. After many struggles with Golcondah, they were driven out of Pencondah to Chundergiri, a strong fortress to the eastward, and lost all their dominions to the north and north-west. Some of their vicissitudes can be traced in the history of Mysore, and show occasional vigour in the representatives of the dynasty, and attempts to recover their position. One of these efforts gave them possession of Anagoondy and a portion of their old dominions; but the Mahrattas and Tippoo Sooltan prevented, most effectually, the existence of any independent power except their own. Finally, after the capture of Seringapatam, the possessions of the family were prescribed to the town of Anagoondy and some villages dependent upon it, which were continued by His Highness the Nizam, and a pension of 1500 rupees per month was allowed by the British government, which is still enjoyed. Mr. Ravenshaw's genealogy shows a succession of eighteen princes, from Rama Rajah in 1564 to Veer Venketpati Rama in 1829, completing a list of 122 from the earliest record: rejecting, therefore, the untraceable early portion, and the insignificant condition of the latter, the powerful portion of the dynasty had existed from A.D. 1334 to 1565, or 231 years, and, until the great combination against it, had not only defied the utmost efforts of the Mahomedans, but had successfully prevented any extension of their dominions to the southward.

TABLE OF THE BEEJANUGGUR DYNASTY.

Mr. H. H. Wilson's Chronological Statement.	A.D.		A.D.
Bukka Raya	1313	to	1327
Harihara	1327	,,	1341
Vijaya	1341	,,	1354
Viswadéva	1354	,,	1362
Ráma Deva	1362	,,	1369
Virupáksha	1369	,,	1374
Mallikárjuna	1374	,,	1381
Ramachandra	1381	,,	1390
Sáluva Ganda	1390	,,	1397
Deva Raya	1396	,,	1412
Kumbhaya	1412	,,	1417
Kumára	1417	,,	1421
Saruvaa Ganda II.	1421	,,	1428
Saruvaa Narasimha	1428	,,	1477
Immadi Deva	1477	,,	1488
Vira Narasimha	1488	,,	1509
Krishna Deva	1509	,,	1529
Achutya	1529	,,	1542
Sadasiva	1542	,,	1564
Trimala	1564	,,	1572
Sri Ranga	1572	,,	1586
Venketapati	1586	,,	1615
Sri Ranga II.	1615	,,	1628
Venkata	1628	,,	1636
Ráma Deva	1636	,,	1643
Anagundi Venketapati	1643	,,	1655
Sri Ranga III.	1655	,,	1655
	352 years.		

Mr. Ravenshaw's Genealogy.	A.D.
Bukka	1334
Harihara	1367
Deva Rai	1391
Vijaya Rai	1414
Pundara Deva Rai	1424
Ramchandra	1450
Narsimha Raja	1395
Vira Narsimha Raja	1490
Achuta Rai	—
Krishna Deva Maha Raya	1524
Rama Raja	1564
Sri Ranga Raja	1568
Trimala Raja	Uncertain.
Vira Yangatpati	
Sri Ranga Raja	
Rama Deva Rai	
Venketpati Rai	
Trimala Rai	
Rama Deva Rai	
Sri Ranga Rai	
Venketpati	
Rama Râi	
Hari Das	1693
Chakdas	1704
Chima Das	1727
Rama Raya	1734
Gopal Rai	—
Yankatpati	1741
Trimal Rai	1756

Mackenzie Collection.—Dates of Inscriptions.	A.D.		A.D.
Bukka	1370	to	1375
Harihara	1385	,,	1429
Deva Raja	1426	,,	1458
Mullicarjuna	1451	,,	1468
Virúpaksha	1473	,,	1479
Nara Sinha	1487	,,	1508
Krishna	1508	,,	1530
Achutya	1530	,,	1542
Sada Siva	1542	,,	1570
Trimala	1568	,,	1571
Sriranga	1574	,,	1584
Venketpati	1587	,,	1608
Virarama	1622	,,	1626

II. MYSORE.

THE History of Mysore is one of many states, large and small, which rose into existence after the destruction of Beejanuggur, and the removal of the successive members of its dynasty to Pencondah, Chundergiri, and Vellore. The Hindoo government of Beejanuggur was formed, as all ancient Hindoo administrations were, more upon a feudal than a centralizing principle. The Mahomedans rejected the feudal system as long as it was possible for them to maintain direct authority over all parts of their dominions; and it was a sure sign of local decrease of power and vigour, in fact of the approaching dismemberment of a Mahomedan state, when it reverted to primitive Hindoo usages. Thus, as Colonel Wilks observes, "the external appearance of the Government of Beejanuggur was brilliant and imposing: its internal "organization feeble and irregular; and foreign conquest was a more fashionable theme than domestic finance "at the court; and while the expulsion of the Mussulmans from the Deccan was chanted by the bards, as an "exploit already achieved, the disorganized state of the distant provinces, would have announced, to a judicious "observer, the approaching dissolution of the empire."

The traditions of the Mysore family attribute its rise, at a very remote period, from two of the Yádavas of Guzerat, who, wandering through the south of India, reached the little fort of Hadana, near Mysore; and one of them, having chivalrously rescued a damsel, the daughter of the "Wadyar," or local petty chieftain, from a marriage to which she objected, married her himself, and became lord of two townships, Hadana and Caroogully. From him, in lineal descent, Chám Raj reigned in A.D. 1507. By this time the family had acquired some local standing and territory; and a subsequent Rajah, Betád Cham Raj, at his death, made a division of his possessions among his three sons, of whom one of them, also named Cham Raj, became possessed of Mysore and its dependencies, and a fort was built there in or about A.D. 1534. These three families have in turn supplied successors and wives to all the reigning Mysore princes; but the separation of territory did not continue.

The fall of Beejanuggur, it will be remembered, occurred in 1565, and although the northern provinces soon afterwards ceased to belong to the State, it still possessed those to the southward and eastward, into which the Mahomedans did not penetrate for nearly a century later. One of these was Mysore; and in 1571, Heeree Chám Raj succeeded to its government, under a viceroy of the kingdom, who resided at Seringapatam, only ten miles from Mysore. It may be supposed, exclusive of his authority as a small provincial governor of the Hindoo state, that, according to the custom of the times, Chám Raj, "The Great," had gradually enlarged the territory of his family, and was in a position to take advantage of the prevailing distraction of the paramount government; for he is described as evading payment of the state revenue or tribute due to the Viceroy, fortifying Mysore, and escaping from an attempt made by the Viceroy to apprehend him; and thus defying the authority of the government, he finally established his own authority about the period of the capture of Beejanuggur. This person died in 1576, leaving no issue; and a cousin, Betad Wadyar, was selected by the family and dependants as his successor. In two years, however, the finances of the little State had fallen into disorder, and the Viceroy's demands were most likely renewed without the possibility of evasion; for the elders of the family and the heads of the soldiery, deposed Betád Wadyar, and elected another cousin, Raj Wadyar; when the arrear due to government—5000 pagodas, or 1840*l.*—being raised, partly from among the family and partly among their dependants, and paid, the Viceroy recognized the new arrangement and sanctioned it. "Wadyar" was a local title in Mysoor, and signified lord of thirty-three villages. The whole of the country appears to have been divided into these petty baronies; and, as a consequence, perpetual feuds and quarrels on all sorts of pretences were the result. Those who were strong, rich, and active, maintained their authority; those who were poor, peaceful, or apathetic, lost it. The family of Mysore seem to have exerted their hereditary warlike tendencies, and to have acquired several of these "Wadyar" divisions, and also to have forced their neighbours to obey them; for in 1610 Raj Wadyar had sufficient influence to obtain possession of the fort and dependencies of Seringapatam, and to oblige the Viceroy to retire. Forty-six years had elapsed since the downfall of Beejanuggur. The attempt to reinstate it at Pencondah had failed, and the family had retreated to their last stronghold, Chundragiri, not far from the eastern coast. From the capital, therefore, the Viceroy, himself aged and worn out, could expect no assistance; and as no violence is recorded, he appears to have made the best bargain he could with Raj Wadyar, and given him peaceable possession of the fort. Seringapatam was then, as it yet is, a considerable town, and was supported, not only by being the seat of a vice-royalty, but by the temple of Sri Rúnga (Vishnu) which, originally built by the Bellál kings of Dwára Samoodra, or by the Cholas of Kunchi, still remained a sacred place of pilgrimage. Henceforward the family of Mysore, heretofore Wadyars only, assumed a higher station as Rajahs; and to accommodate themselves to the spirit of the time, changed their creed. They had hitherto belonged to the Monotheistic faith of the Jungums, which had arisen at the end of the Chalúkya dynasty, about the beginning of the twelfth century; but in so holy a place as the precincts of "Sri Runga" (Krishna, an avatar of Vishnu) the simple puritanic and heretical Jungum dissent could not hope for the countenance of Brahmins, and Raj Wadyar, accommodating his belief to his circumstances, entered the pale of the Brahminical faith, and became a votary of "Sri Ranga." Subsequently, about 1687, this faith was publicly professed by a descendant; but until then the Jungum creed of Chun Bussappa was not entirely forsaken by the family. Henceforward, however, the growth of territory progressed; and in the two following successions, Chám Raj and Immádi Raj, the little State had considerably advanced, though in the latter reigns the "Dulwey," or minister, had already usurped all the executive power. It is probably more to this cause that the growth and progress of Hindoo kingdoms may be attributed, than to the personal exertions of the sovereigns. Themselves for the most part vain, arrogant, and sensual, sunk in luxury or debauchery, their affairs were left to ministers who, while they advanced their own power, maintained their princes as mere pageants, and did not hesitate to remove them by restraint or murder, when they displayed activity, or were no longer subservient. Thus Immádi Raj, who had evinced some promise, was soon destroyed, and Canta Dèva Mahá Rajah installed as his successor. By this time, A.D. 1654, the Mahomedan kings of Beejapoor had prosecuted their conquests to the south, and Rend Dhoola Khan, an officer of the army of

Mahmood Adil Shah of Beejapoor, attacked Seringapatam, and demanded the tribute paid to the Rajahs of Beejanuggur. This demand, however, was stoutly resisted: and the Mahomedan general's troops were repulsed with great slaughter from a breach which he had made in the fort walls. The siege was not only raised, but he was pursued on his retreat, and severely handled. Canteraya Rajah seems to have been little disposed to submit to the domination of any minister. He took the direction of affairs into his own hands, rearranged the revenue assessments, subdued all refractory vassals, improved the fortifications of his capital, and, the first of his race, established a mint and coined money in his own name. The coin known as "Canterai Pagodas" still bears his name. Sree Runga, the great idol of Seringapatam, received from him "a crown of jewels;" all temples were re-endowed, and, as a patron of Brahmins, he advanced, in their estimation, over all his predecessors. The homely usages of his family were exchanged for the etiquette of a regal court, and the little state of Mysore soon emerged from its obscurity into the full light of political existence. The record of this reign furnishes a long list of annexations and booties the result of Canteráya's petty wars with his neighbours, whose properties were joined to his own as fast as small predatory expeditions could be organized, or pretext for quarrel established.

The next reign, that of Dud Deo Raj, or Déo Raj the Great, is remarkable for an attempt by a prince of the ancient Beejanuggur house to recover Seringapatam and the western portion of the territory of his ancestors. The family by this time had further declined, and were obliged to give up Chandergiri and Vellore to the Mahomedans, when Sree Runga Rayeel fled from Vellore and took refuge with the Rajah of Bednoor, who, a former vassal, had long been independent; but now availed himself of the presence of a descendant of the royal house to attempt conquests in his name. In this instance, however, no benefit resulted: but the contrary, for the Bednoor army retreated, and the Mysore prince, whether by conquest, or by extortion, or both, became possessed of several new provinces to the northward and westward. Out of the ruins of Beejanuggur, too, had risen another southern State, that of Madura, formerly belonging to the Pandyan dynasty, whose territories, like Mysore, were being increased by conquests. Its Rajah, or Naik, contemplated the annexation of Mysore, and even attempted it; but was defeated, losing Bangalore, then partly fortified, the impregnable rock of Savendroog, and other valuable territory on the table-land. From the list of acquisitions, also, in the reign of Déo Raj the Great, it appears that by this time (1667) the Mysore territory had extended considerably below the plateau to the south, and to the north as far as the old Hindoo capital of Hullabeed, or Dwára Samoodra.

Before the appearance of the Moghuls of Dehli in the south of India, and most especially before the subdivision of the Deccan kingdoms by Aurungzeeb and the Mahratta power, the south of India would appear to have been divided pretty nearly as follows. The Adil Shahy kingdom, under Mahmood Adil Shah and his successor, Ali Adil Shah II, possessed authority as far south as Bangalore, Vellore, and Ginjee, from which the Chola Hindoo princes had been expelled; and from Bangalore, in a north-west direction, to Pencondah and Bednoor. Northwards, Beejapoor had lost some of its ancient dominions; and it is very questionable whether its southern conquests, though nominally much larger, were ever decisive ; for until the final subversion of the capital by Aurungzeeb, the Beejapoor armies were constantly engaged in hostilities to the south, which, so far from strengthening, considerably weakened the kingdom, both in troops and in the cost of their maintenance. Mysore, as has been shown, had now established itself as a political state of some power; and there were besides, the Näiks or Rajahs of Ginjee, of Tanjore, Madura, Chennapatnam (Madras), Chingleput, &c, held by Jugdeo Rayeel, a member of the Beejanuggur family, and its last southern possession. The Rayeels, when finally expelled from the eastward, about 1646, had made some further attempts, besides those directed against Seringapatam, to regain the western portion of their ancient dominions, including Bednoor and Coorg; but, as has been already stated, without avail. There were also Poligars of Chittuldroog, Rai Droog, Hurpunhullee, Tarikera, Mudun Séra, Rutnagiri, &c, north of Mysore, who owned a nominal allegiance to Beejanuggur as the strongest party, but were in fact marauders, living by plunder, and levying black mail wherever they had power enough to do so. The whole presents to the imagination a confused and seething mass of conflicting interests and endeavours, wherein the only right was that of the strongest; when every petty or great authority, from the owner of a village to that of a principality, was in arms against his neighbour, and men rose or fell, according as they possessed local power, or the ability to maintain, or good fortune to extend it. Collectively unable to oppose the Mahomedan progress in the most trifling degree: singly, mischievous and predatory, the Hindoo

States, with the exception of Mysore, gradually disappeared before the Mahomedans—first of Beejapoor, and afterwards of the Imperial invasion. As the ancient kingdoms of Chóla and Pandú had disappeared before the predatory efforts of the Rayeels of Beejanuggur, so in turn also their successors, who have been mentioned, were absorbed in the Mahomedan and Mahratta conquests.

Chik Déo Raj, or Déo Raj the Less, did not succeed his cousin till he was forty-five years old; Déo Raj the Great had left no issue, and he was elected as the next in blood. Up to the period of his accession the new prince had been poor; and it is almost strange to find among Hindoo princes, the experience of adversity aiding the progress of prosperity. Déo Raj the Less proved an astute ruler. His dominions were out of the way, as it were, of the successive waves of Mahomedan and Mahratta invasion, and were passed by unscathed; and this circumstance left the Rajah time to improve and consolidate his internal administration. For the first time in India we find a post-office was established, for neither the Mahomedans nor Hindoos of the elder dynasties ever appear to have organized or used such a means of public intercourse; the regulation of finance and general management of departments was efficiently maintained; and the administration in all respects appears to have been eminently regular and practical. Politically, the Rajah professed subservience to Aurungzeeb; but it does not appear that he ever paid tribute. The annual revenues of the Mysoor State now amounted to 1,323,571 pagodas (about 500,000*l.*), and there were nine millions of pagodas (about three millions sterling) in the treasury. From 1610 to 1700, therefore, or in ninety years, the State had gradually progressed to its maximum through the stormy period of the seventeenth century.

It could hardly be supposed, in those lawless times, that the reputed possession of such riches would not attract either the Mahrattas, the Imperial Moghul commanders, or the Patán Nawábs who, gathering together Affghans from the north, with the descendants of the Beejapoor and Ahmednuggur armies, had already formed some independent states out of the old Hindoo materials. The principal of these were the Nawábs of Kurpa (Cuddapa), Kurnool, and Savanoor; and in 1724 the Rajah of Mysore was obliged to pay a million sterling as ransom for his State, conjointly to them and to the Mahrattas of Gooty. This did not, however, impair the resources of his principality, which seem to have been recruited by like acts of exaction or plunder in other directions to the south and west; and while it escaped alike from the Mahrattas, now established at Gooty, Tanjore, and Ginjee, and from the Soobah of the Deccan, Nizam-ool-Moolk, it maintained a consistent prosperity and tranquillity, at that period very rare. The princes themselves were in no degree remarkable, except in some instances for excessive depravity and sensuality; but there were always wise and efficient ministers to conduct public affairs with respectability, and, on the whole, Mysore presents at this period the picture of a well governed and prosperous Hindoo State, very well able to protect its own interests.

It would exceed the province of this memoir to enter into any detail of the wars in which the French and English, the Mahrattas, Mahomedans, and the Rajah of Mysore, contended for the supremacy of the south of India; but during these wars, Hyder Ali, who had risen, by his intelligence and bravery, to the rank of "Foujdar," or commander-in-chief of the Mysore army, now became a prominent public character. Nundé Raj, the minister of Mysore, the Rajah himself being little more than a pageant, was an able man; but to control Hyder,—who, following the example of the Mahrattas, had organized a very remarkable, and, as it soon came to be, a most formidable system of predatory warfare and plunder of all surrounding states,—was beyond his power. Large bodies of Beydurs, who were the hereditary freebooters of south-western India, were entertained, both horse and foot, by Hyder Ali; and his whole organization, if it were not constructed on the actual model of Sivajee Rajah who had founded the Mahratta power by similar means, was at least as formidable and as destructive. During Hyder's absence on his first campaign, a domestic revolution had occurred at Seringapatam; and the Rajah, resenting the condition in which he had been placed, and the conduct of his brothers, and narrowly escaping from a design by Nundé Raj to destroy him, suddenly left the capital with some faithful adherents, and repaired to Sattimungalum, a town below the Mysore plateau in the southern district of Coimbatoor. He would have been pursued, and most likely destroyed by the minister, but at this juncture was saved by an irruption of Mahrattas, under Balajee Rao, who demanded the Chouth and Surdeshmookhee of Sivajee. These claims being refused, they laid siege to Seringapatam, and relinquished their operations only on promise of payment of thirty-two lacs of rupees (320,000*l.*), for which fifteen districts were pledged, the minister professing to be too poor to pay the amount in cash. Hyder Ali, who returned to the capital, was unable to pursue them, but soon after effected a reconciliation between the Rajah and his brothers, and induced him to revisit Seringapatam, as the only means of averting further disorganization of the State. The Rajah, however, only survived his return a few days; he died of dropsy, or, by some accounts, of poison, within a week of his arrival, and was succeeded by his brother. Without any satisfaction of their claims, or fulfilment of promises, the Mahrattas had been expelled from the pledged districts, and in 1759 they re-invaded Mysore, and regained them. A campaign followed, in which Hyder Ali proved successful in the field, and the Mahrattas eventually surrendered their claim to the disputed territory, but only on payment of the original thirty-two lacs of rupees; and thereupon, for the present, departed northwards. This service to the State increased the power of Hyder Ali very materially, and he was granted the title of "Futteh Bahádur," "the valiant in victory;" but the removal of the minister, Nundé Raj, was necessary to the completion of his ambitious plans, and after pressure had been put on him to provide means for payment of the troops, then heavily in arrears, he resigned his office, to which Hyder Ali, now supreme in all executive affairs, appointed his own agent and minister, Khundé Rao. This having been confirmed by the Rajah, the confederates obtained from him assignments of districts for the payment of the army, which comprised more than half the State dominions. When all these preliminary arrangements had been concluded, Hyder Ali received an invitation from the French to assist them against theEnglish; and he entered upon the campaign which ensued with his accustomed impetuosity and vigour. Into these transactions it is impossible to enter; but it became evident to the Dowager Queen of Mysore, that in displacing Nundé Raj, a more powerful, dangerous, and ambitious servant had usurped the State authority. Accordingly, having, under an oath of secresy, unfolded her purposes to Khundé Rao, she succeeded in separating him from Hyder's interest, and attaching him to the Rajah's cause. By Khundé Rao's means, the services of a large body of Mahratta horse were now engaged; and on their arrival at Seringapatam, Hyder Ali, who had returned to the capital, was suddenly attacked, and, after an ineffectual defence, obliged to fly, leaving the public affairs, the army, and all military stores in the hands of his former servant.

But Hyder Ali's fortunes were not altogether desperate. He had friends, not only among the Mahomedan tributary chiefs of the State, but among the bankers; and after a series of struggles and expedients, he once more ascended the plateau of Mysore with a considerable force, and met Khundé Rao near the village of Nunjengode. In this engagement, however, he was defeated with heavy loss. Hyder then left his army, rode with a small detachment of horse, seventy of whom were French hussars, to Cunnoor, where Nundé Raj resided, threw himself at his feet, and implored his protection, beseeching him at the same time to resume his office. Nundé Raj consented, and letters were forthwith written to all authorities apprising them of the new coalition. Among these documents Hyder adroitly caused some to be addressed to the officers of Khundé Rao's army, which, purporting to agree with their plans for deposing the minister and throwing him into Hyder's power, he contrived should fall into the hands of Khundé Rao himself. This ruse had exactly the effect intended; for Khundé Rao, conceiving himself surrounded by treachery, mounted his horse in a sudden panic, and fled. Hyder had meanwhile rejoined his own forces, which were near the royal troops, and observing confusion among them, owing to the flight of their commander, attacked them fiercely, and obtained a complete victory, all their guns and material of war falling into his hands. He did not follow up his success, and to all appearance retreated; but on receipt of information that the fugitives had collected together and were encamped carelessly, he turned, fell upon them at midnight, and slew great numbers of them. As yet, however, he was not strong enough to attack Seringapatam; but this was not long delayed, and in May 1771, having called in all his forces, he marched on the capital. Khundé Rao's troops were encamped under its walls; but by a sudden attack they were dispersed, and it only remained for Hyder Ali to dictate terms to his master the Rajah. They were hard enough. The Rajah's own proposal after some discussion, was, to retain districts yielding three lacs (30,000*l.*) per year, for his own support, and to give up everything else to Hyder, including Khundé Rao. It would have been merciful had he been executed; instead of this he was sent to Bangalore, and confined for the remainder of his wretched life in an iron cage, as Hyder said, "like a parrot," and fed daintily," being a Brahmin, upon rice and milk. The whole of this transaction is a grim romance, played out with unmitigated fraud and deceit on both sides. It may well be supposed that Khundé Rao's treachery to Hyder Ali could only have originated in his own ambitious designs for usurpation; and the issue shows, in their true colours, as well the ingenious perseverance, as the cruel and relentless character of the conqueror.

Henceforth the princely family of Mysore existed but in name, and as a pageant attached to the State of which Hyder Ali was now supreme. In all his future campaigns and political negotiations he acted on his own behalf, and for the kingdom he had virtually won. Gradually his forces overran the whole of the northern provinces, establishing his frontier as far as the Tumboodra, and driving out the Mahrattas and the Nizam, who possessed them. Gooty, held by Morari Rao, and Bednore followed. This was a wild, woody country, with few practicable routes through it; but Hyder penetrated to the capital, which was surprised, and the terrified inhabitants having fled to the mountains around, all the public and private property fell into the conqueror's hands. It was the accumulation of many ages; and, as Colonel Wilkes records, was not less than twelve millions sterling, which laid the foundation of all his future greatness. The Ranee, who, after setting fire to the palace, had fled to "Bellál Raidroog," surrendered herself; and, with her paramour, who had been her minister, was imprisoned in the hill fort of Mudgherri, where she remained till released by the Mahrattas in 1767. Another tragedy, however, had to be enacted before his conquest was complete. Hyder fell ill of fever before he could leave Bednoor, and was reported dying, when the adherents of the old dynasty formed a conspiracy for his assassination. This he discovered; and on the same day upwards of three hundred of the conspirators were hung at different points of the city. Henceforth he held undisturbed possession of the Bednoor territory: but there his army suffered terribly from the climate, and the Mahrattas, under Mahdoo Rao Péshwah, attacked him before he could release himself from his position. Hyder suffered a bloody defeat, and his treasure, in being removed by secret passes through the woods and hills, very narrowly escaped capture. Eventually he was obliged to ask for terms, and to accept what were granted. These were the relinquishment of the territory of Gooty, and of all claims against Savanoor, with the payment of thirty-two lacs (320,000*l.*) as chouth and expenses of the war. It was then perfectly possible for the Mahrattas to have pressed him to unconditional surrender; and had Mahdoo Rao been aware of the amount of treasure almost within his grasp, there is little doubt he would have made a strenuous effort to obtain it. Hyder's good fortune, however, befriended him, and from this, the turning-point of his wonderful career, he can hardly be said to have sustained a reverse. Into the succeeding wars with the English, the Nizam, and the Mahrattas; his acquisitions in Canara and Malabar; and into the results of his political policy and internal government, it is not the province of this memoir to enter: and they have already become the material of several brilliant and instructive histories. Henceforward he acted as an independent monarch, and termed his State Khodá-dád, the "Gift of God;" but nevertheless, and almost in a spirit of bitter mockery, he preserved the royal race, of which he still declared himself a servant, after the manner of the Péshwahs of Poona, who had acted in a similar spirit in regard to the descendants of Sivajee. In April 1766, the old Rajah, Chik Kishen Raj Wadyar died, and his son Nundi Raj was immediately invested with the royal dignity. He was eighteen years of age, and began to evince a spirit of inquiry, restlessness, and impatience which could not be endured. He was therefore closely confined; the districts which had been settled on his father were resumed, and his palace plundered—not only of money, but of every article of gold or silver convertible into money, except the few ornaments worn by the women. Five years afterwards, however, the young man, unable to endure patiently the indignities from which he suffered, made a vain attempt at communication with Trimbuk Rao, General of the Mahrattas. This was detected, and Hyder, no longer considering him safe, ordered him to be strangled in his bath; after which his brother Cham Raj was nominated to succeed him. This Prince seems to have lived in utter obscurity, for no mention is further made of him until his death, which occurred in 1775. On that occasion, as the direct lineal male succession was extinct, Hyder assembled all the male children of the collateral branches, and, according to an ancient Hindoo custom, set them to play in a hall strewed with playthings, arms, ornaments, bags of money, and the like, in order to watch, as a kind of divination, what each would take up, and to decide the succession accordingly. While the rest were playing or scrambling for toys and sweetmeats, a boy took up a dagger. "That is the Rajah," exclaimed Hyder, "his first care is military protection, his second, to realize the produce of his dominions; "bring him hither, and let me embrace him;" and a murmur of applause followed. This boy was also named Chám Raj, and was father of the present Rajah.

During the war with the English in 1782, Hyder Ali died, in the month of November, of a virulent cancer or carbuncle in his back, and was succeeded by his son Tippoo, who assumed the title of "Sultán,"from which his father had refrained. The general reader is referred to Colonel Wilks's "History of Mysore," vol. iii.

for an able analysis of Hyder's character, which is too extended to admit of quotation. Perhaps he may be more nearly compared with Sivajee the Mahratta, both in unscrupulous cunning and audacious bravery, than with any other Indian character of history; but Sivajee was essentially the most merciful, as he was the most honourable, of the two. Sivajee created a new power by his own indomitable spirit to overthrow one which was oppressive to the people of his country; whereas Hyder's rise was founded entirely upon the worst features of treachery and usurpation. Sivajee was not habitually cruel, though his character is stained by some bloody and vindictive deeds; but Hyder was cold-blooded, and unsafe even to his nearest friends and, outwardly, most favoured dependants. His fearful system of espionage, which penetrated to every family, left no one secure from death or horrible mutilation at any moment; and with him human suffering, while it appeared to give no pleasure, was accompanied by no regret or sympathy. Both used predatory power as a means of territorial acquisition; but in Sivajee's hands this was more formidably wielded than in Hyder's, and more successfully, considering the superiority of the Moghul armies over any, except the English, with which Hyder came in contact. Sivajee's more generous disposition shared public counsels with his friends: and of his deep affection for his devoted adherents Tannajee Maloosray and Netajee Pálkar, and for many others, there are too many proofs to be doubted for a moment. Hyder, on the contrary, never had a friend; nor did human affection seem to exist in him in the least degree. "He had no adviser," writes Colonel Wilks, "and no confidant. He encouraged on all occasions free discussion of every measure suggested by himself or "others, but no person knew at its close what measures he would adopt in consequence." In his harem were six hundred women, and yet for no one member of it does he seem to have evinced the least regard or love. But of the mother of his son Tippoo he was afraid: she had a long tongue, he said; and his best historian and biographer, Meer Hussun Ali Khan Kermani, gives, with naive gravity, many amusing instances of his sharp passages with her. It is impossible to accuse a Mahomedan biographer of injustice to one who was the theme of his most inflated panegyric; and a few passages may be quoted from the Meer's work, which, although translated by Colonel Miles, is perhaps very little known. "His (Hyder Ali's) court was magnificent," writes the Meer, "but, except himself, few dared to speak therein. Whatever he desired to be done, he himself "ordered, and the rest of the assembly had no choice but to give their assent. . . . All the operations or "measures undertaken by his government, small or great, were superintended by himself in person, insomuch, "that even leather, the lining of bullock bags, or tent walls, and strands of rope, all passed under his "inspection. . . . . His estimate of the value of the brave and experienced soldier, of whatever tribe or caste "he might be, was very high; and any man who had distinguished himself by his bravery he heartily cherished "and protected. . . . He was, however, the enemy of the indolent and luxurious, and the backs and sides of "his negligent and extortionate servants were frequently softened by stripes of the whip." No one convicted of extortion, peculation, or other misdemeanour, was ever restored to office, and in every department were spies and secret writers, by whose means "he acquired a knowledge of every act of his servants, good or bad." "He "went out often by night covered with a blanket, both in camp and in his capital, and ascertained the condition "of the people, and the rumours or opinions regarding himself. He was constantly in the field, and enjoyed "movement; the delight given by new scenery, or a new ground of encampment, fresh springs and the "grateful shade of the tent, did he ever forego." Hyder could neither write nor read; as a signature to public documents, all he could effect was the initial letter of his name: but after much labour in copying it, he always wrote it the wrong way: his wonderful memory, however, supplied the want of learning.

Another native biographer, Mirza Ikbal, gives, if possible, more graphic and familiar accounts of Hyder Ali. "When the Rajah of Mysore was deposed, he began to raise the head of pride. By degrees he became "strange and forgetful, requiring obeisances and respectful observances. Towards the end of his reign he "abandoned all consideration for any persons, however respectable; he gave them the vilest abuse, and for the "least fault put them to death. In his durbars, or levées, no one dared converse or even whisper. If any one "had a wedding in his house he could not invite friends, except through the Nawab, or the agency of his "servants." Even then spies were sent to see and report what was done. "If he confided to any one the "charge of a district, God protect him if he took to the value of a blade of grass beside the dues assigned to "him, he was sure to be flayed alive. If he took any and it was found out, the money was demanded; and if "paid, well: but if it were not, he was seized and tied with ropes, like a horse, before and behind, and having "been stripped naked, an order was given to flay him with a whip, and a number of 'gowal dóz' beat him "cruelly over the back and loins; after which salt was thrown upon his wounds. If he cried, red pepper, "dried and powdered, was thrown into his eyes." Besides this, if he did not pay the money, "iron spits or rods "were made red hot, and he was burned or branded all over."

This account is corroborated by the letter of the Rev. Mr. Schwartz, who, a missionary in the south of India, visited Seringapatam on an errand of peace from the Madras Government in 1779-80. "Here reigns no "pomp," he writes, "but the utmost regularity and dispatch; although Hyder sometimes rewards his servants, "yet their principal motive is fear. Two hundred people with whips always stand ready to use them. Not a "day passes in which numbers are not flogged. Hyder applies the same cat to all transgressors alike—gentlemen "and horse-keepers, tax-gatherers and his own sons. . . . I hardly know whether I shall mention how one "of these gentlemen was punished. Many who read it may think the account exaggerated; but the poor man "was tied up; two men came with their whips and cut him dreadfully; with sharp nails was his flesh torn "asunder, and then scourged afresh. His shrieks rent the air. Hyder has spies everywhere; the most intimate "friends dare not speak their sentiments freely." The whole of the account of this visit is replete with interesting matter; but in the present case the native record may be more suitable.

Hyder would remember a word for years, and never forgot a face he had once seen. "Once he desired the "overseer of his stables to bring an old saddle; it was brought. 'Not that,' said the Nawab; 'it is a Mahratta "'saddle, with a lining of yellow broadcloth, moth-eaten. I desired it should be wrapped in a cloth and taken "'care of.' The saddle was found, and the order had been given eleven years before. Personally, he was plain, "and 'free from vanity.' He was not fond of delicacies, and 'ate what they set before him.' In his dress also "he was equally plain. 'His vest was of white calico, and his trowsers of Masulipatam chintz—a white ground "'with red flowers on it. He slept on a silken carpet, and this, with two or three pillows, were all he required "'for his bed.'"

As a Mahomedan, Hyder was tolerant beyond any known professor of the faith, except perhaps Akbar, Emperor of Dehli. He never interfered with his Hindoo subjects, and never attempted their conversion, which became so brutal an instrument of oppression in his son. "Hyder believed," as Colonel Wilks records, "that "all religions proceed from God, and all are equal in the sight of God; and it is certain that the mediatory "power represented by Runga Swámi, the great idol in the temple at Seringapatam, had as much, if not more "of his respect, than all the Imams, with Mahomed at his head." Colonel Wilks confirms the account given of Hyder's relations with those who served him. "It was a calculation," he writes, "whether it were most "beneficial to plunder or to employ them. Everything was weighed in the balance of utility, and no grain of "human feeling, no breath of virtue or of vice—was permitted to incline the beam. . . . There was but one "solitary example of feeling incident to our nature, affection for an unworthy son, whom he nominated to be "his successor, while uniformly, earnestly, and broadly predicting that he would lose the empire which he him-"self had gained." The scene of his death-bed, as given by Meer Hussein Ali, is characteristic. "The Nawab "directed that water might be made ready for him to bathe, and although the physicians objected to his "bathing, they (the servants) turned them out of the tent, and the Nawab bathed. Then, having put on clean "clothes, he repeated some prayer or invocation on his finger; rubbing his face, and, at the same time, "dispatched some two thousand horse to plunder and ravage the country of the Poligars, and five thousand "horse to Madras for the same purpose, . . . then he took a little broth, and lay down to rest. That same "night his ever-victorious spirit took its flight to paradise." A grim exit from life, truly, with its "ruling "passion strong in death." Once more would his cavalry ravage unoffending Hindoo villages and bring in their plunder. Once more would the hated English of Madras see around their fort the tall columns of smoke of burning villages.

Tippoo Sultan, his son, died bravely in defence of his own capital, on the 2nd of May, 1799. He had reigned seventeen years amidst perpetual turmoil, cruelty, spoliation, and intrigue, of which his subjects were weary, and which had become dangerous to the peace of India. Perhaps the best estimate of his character is given by one of his own confidential servants, Syud Hussein, in a record which is quoted by Colonel Wilks. "There was nothing," writes the Syud, "of permanency in his views, no solidity in his "councils, and no confidence on the part of the governed. All was innovation on his part, and the fear of "further novelty on the part of others; and the order of to-day was expected to be reversed by the invention "of to-morrow. It may be affirmed of his principal measures, that, however specious, all had a tendency to "injure the finances, to undermine the government, and oppress the people. All the world was puzzled "what distinct character should be assigned to a sovereign who was never the same. He could neither be "truly characterized as liberal nor parsimonious, as tyrannical nor benevolent, as a man of talent nor as destitute "of parts. By turns he assumed the character of each. . . . The most intelligent and sincere well-wishers "of the house concurred in the opinion of his father, that his head and heart were both defective, however "covered by a plausible and imposing flow of words, and that they were not always without symptoms of "mental aberration."

Such were the two men, father and son, who had for thirty-five years usurped the power and the dominions of Mysore, and greatly extended both. They were equally unprincipled; but Hyder had a clear, undisturbed view of the interests of ambition; in Tippoo that view was incessantly obscured and perverted by the meanest passions. Hyder's views invariably promoted his political interests; Tippoo's more frequently defeated them. Finally, as the Mysore proverb expresses it—"Hyder was born to create a kingdom, Tippoo "to lose one." It is difficult, perhaps, to say whether father or son most excelled in deliberate cruelty. Hyder in his was cold-blooded, methodical, and seldom capricious. Robbers, thieves, corrupt police and revenue officers and agents, frequently prisoners of war, especially Mahrattas, were impaled, hanged, flayed alive, mutilated, or had merely noses and ears cut off. His object was to strike terror into enemies and evil-doers, and it had at least a public object; for his subjects, though often trembling themselves, felt the assurance of his vigorous hand in the executive government. Hyder did not commit useless murders. This was reversed in his son, whose never-ending mutilations, forcible conversions, and secret and vindictive murders, even of his captives, accompanied a weak executive, which, out of the very measures taken to strengthen it, only grew weaker every day. Of no native government in India, not even of the Punjab, have we such complete, true, and graphic pictures as of Mysore under Hyder and his son. No perversion of local transactions could be accomplished, even were it desired; and alike from Tippoo Sultan's own and the daily records of official transactions of the period, as from French, English, and native biographers and journalists, are the particulars of these reigns left without doubt or concealment. May they not be recalled, hideous as they are, to be contrasted with the peace and security of what has existed since their destruction up to the present time?

It will be remembered that there had been a Rajah, Nundi Raj, elevated to the dignity by Hyder Ali in 1772, who had been immediately placed in close confinement, and was afterwards strangled. His successor, Chám Raj, died of smallpox in 1796. By Tippoo, as well as by his father, this wretched prince had been shewn to the Hindoo people of Mysore at every Dussera, and on the present occasion a repetition of the ceremony of succession was expected. None, however, took place. The deceased's heir was a boy of two years old, and, with his mother and grandmother, were removed from their palace to a hovel. Then the palace was once more rifled of what little it contained, and even the personal ornaments did not on this occasion escape. "The Rajah cried bitterly," writes Colonel Wilks, "at the attempt to take away his little golden "bracelets, and there was still sufficient feeling among the instruments of tyranny to be touched at the distress "of the child, and to abstain from this last violation." Not very long afterwards, in November 1787, Tippoo, considering the town and fort of Mysore to be an offensive memorial of the ancient family, determined to obliterate as far as possible every vestige of their possessions, and destroyed both. The old fort was levelled with the ground, a new one was constructed with the materials upon a neighbouring height, and the inhabitants of the town were ordered to remove to Seringapatam. "It is a curious example of that vicissitude in "human affairs which history so often preaches in vain," observes Colonel Wilks, "that the very same stones "of the fort were re-conveyed to re-build the same old fort of Mysore in 1799." Notwithstanding the poverty and obscurity of the Rajah's family, the child who survived throve; and when the English victory of Seringapatam ensued, the question remained to be decided whether the sons of Tippoo should inherit a limited territory, or whether the heir of the ancient house should be restored to his ancestral dignity and dominion. The claims of both were discussed anxiously and maturely by the British government of India, "and the "restoration of the descendants of the ancient Rajahs of Mysore," writes Colonel Wilks, 'was recommended "by the same course of reasoning which excluded the heir of the usurpation. The kingdom of Mysore, so long "the source of calamity and alarm, would become a barrier of defence and an accession of strength; and in "addition to these motives of policy, every moral consideration and every sentiment of generosity favoured "the restoration of the Hindoo family of Mysore." The Rajah was therefore installed at the seat of his ancestors, in the presence of an immense multitude of Hindoos, who testified the most unfeigned delight at a spectacle which revived the long extinguished hope of perpetual emancipation from Mahomedan tyranny. Only so much, however, of the Mysore kingdom as had formed the ancient dominions of its last executive Rajah, in the beginning of the century, was confirmed to the new prince. The rest being Hyder's and Tippoo's conquests, were distributed, agreeably with the terms of the tripartite treaty, to His Highness the Nizam, to the Mahrattas, and to the English government, being for the most part their original possessions; but what remained to Mysore was a noble and fertile territory, producing hardly less than a million sterling per year.

The boy thus unexpectedly raised to the throne of Mysore is still alive, and enjoys a green old age of seventy-five years. During his long minority, an able minister, the celebrated "Poornia Dewan," managed the affairs of his State, under the supervision of an English officer resident at the court. Seringapatam was abandoned for Mysore, which was much more salubrious, and was greatly improved as a royal residence. When the Rajah attained his majority, he took possession of a contented, well regulated, and prosperous country, with some millions sterling of accumulated treasure. In a comparatively few years, however, he had squandered the hoards of Poornia in wasteful and profligate extravagance; he had incurred enormous debts, and his dominions became a scene of lawless violence and disorder, for which remonstrance and warning had alike proved ineffectual, and which, no longer endurable, rendered interference imperative. In 1831-32, His Highness the Rajah was, therefore, withdrawn from public affairs, and the country was henceforth governed by a commission of British officers. His vast debts were gradually paid off, and the surplus revenue applied to the improvement of the country at large. By degrees, too, all the former vexatious and oppressive taxation was swept away, and the land revenue settled on a reduced and beneficial system; and there is no province in India perhaps in which the administration has been carried on with purer motives and more beneficial results, than that of Mysore.

His Highness Mahá Rajah Krishna Raj Wadyar Bahadoor has no male issue. He lately applied for permission to adopt an heir and successor to his nominal dominions; but it is generally understood that this has been refused. And considering, indeed, the virtual extinction of all direct lines of descent from the original family, the issue of the request could hardly have been otherwise; while the absolute surrender of the people, so long under the enjoyment of the lightest taxation in India, and the thorough security of a British administration, to the irresponsible and capricious power of a native prince, would, in any case, be a measure of very questionable expediency. There is at least no doubt that every member of the Rajah's family, with the hereditary servants of the State, will be liberally provided for when the Rajah dies; and when, after a troubled, and often precarious existence of 350 years, his dynasty must altogether cease to exist. Maha Rajah Krishna Raj Wadyar is personally a benevolent, hospitable, and courtly personage; a good scholar, and by many accounts a poet also; but gifted with no indication of administrative ability. He possesses, however, a curious and ingenious talent for composing problems of chess, of which he is an accomplished player, combined with arithmetical puzzles. The writer of this memoir was favoured, in 1852, with a specimen of one of these problems, printed on yellow satin, direct from its royal composer—an interesting memorial of one who, in the ordinary course of nature, must soon pass away. For the last seventy years his life has been one of luxurious ease and comfort, and presents a striking and vivid contrast to the miserable degradation and poverty which he would have endured had the dynasty of the Sultan of Mysore continued to exist.

As may perhaps be imagined, there are few remarkable remains of this Hindoo dynasty to perpetuate its existence. The most remarkable of its public works are some irrigation dams and tanks, the stone bridges at Seringapatam and Nunjengode, which, constructed in the monolithic style of Hindoo architecture, are perhaps best able to withstand the tremendous floods of the rivers spanned by them. But the country abounds with noble artificial lakes, and specimens of the purest Hindoo architecture, memorials of the ancient and glorious dynasties of the Hoisála Bellâls of Dwara Samoodra, who were for the most part Jains; and of the Cholas of Kunchi, who were Brahmins: and many of these, still perfect, will be illustrated in this volume.

On a review of the past, the south of India, perhaps, more than the north, presents a view of perpetual strife and change for 300 years preceding the British conquest of Mysore. Even before that, the conquests of the Beejanuggur princes, and the extinction of the ancient Chola and Pandyan kingdoms, which were only gradual, had involved the people in a perpetual series of never-ceasing wars. In the sketch of history which is the subject of this memoir there were not only the Beejanuggur princes at feud with the Mahomedan kings of the Deccan, but those wars were immediately followed by the invasion of the Moghuls of Dehli, and the contests which ensued between the Mahrattas, the Poligars, the English and French, and finally, with Hyder Ali and Tippoo Sultan. But since the beginning of the present century there has been peace, which, under the security of the powerful and beneficent Government of England, has enabled the people, if not to forget the past, at least to marvel how it was endured, and to appreciate the more thankfully those rights and privileges which ensure to them protection, tranquillity, and advancement.

III.

HISTORIC NOTICE OF THE BEYDURS OF HURPUNHULLEE AND CHITTULDROOG.

AFTER the conquest of Beejanuggur, in 1565, by the Mahomedan kings of the Deccan, Ali Adil Shah of Beejapoor, continued the subjugation of the Hindoo districts to the westward and north-westward, which had been held by feudal nobles and viceroys of the Hindoo kingdom. This proved to be by no means an easy task; and the king was materially assisted by the Bergy or Beydur chieftains of northern Mysore, who had joined him after the fall of Beejanuggur, and with whom the Beydur Naik of Sugger, already in the royal service, had been a successful mediator. The possessions of these Beydur chieftains formed a barrier, as it were, against Mahomedan encroachment to the south, extending from the ghauts eastward, as far as Kuddapa. The principal of them were the Poligars of Chittuldroog, Raidroog, Rutnagiri, Hurpunhullee, Tarikéra, Jhellee, &c. and they could at all times command the services of large numbers of their clans, who were brave soldiers, although habitual and hereditary freebooters. In the year 1576-7, Ali Adil Shah made an attempt to drive the Beejanuggur family from Penkonda, where they had retreated; but the reigning prince succeeded in detaching Hundiatum Naik, of Hurpunhullee, the chief of Ali Adil Shah's Beydurs, from him, and he, having united with other chiefs of his tribe, distressed the army of Ali Adil Shah so materially that they forced him to raise the siege and retreat to Bunkapoor. Elated by these successes, the Beydurs generally broke into insurrection; and had any energetic movement on the part of the princes of Beejanuggur followed, it is quite possible that they might have recovered their capital and re-established their dynasty. The king's army could make very little impression upon these wild mountaineers, who defeated or eluded his best troops; at length policy prevailed over force, and the chiefs were guaranteed in their possessions and rights and continued in the royal service till, in its turn, the Mahratta conquest prevailed over the Mahomedan. Such is the earliest record obtainable of the Beydur chiefs in the history of the times; but there is little doubt they were one of the aboriginal tribes of the country: and their clannish attachment and organization, their pursuit of war and plunder as their only occupation, their peculiar tenets and observances, and their innate unchangeable savagery, have always marked them as a race distinct from the ordinary inhabitants.

The Beydur chieftains maintained their positions during the contests between the Mahrattas and the Emperor Aurungzeeb; but their attachment to the Mahrattas, as Hindoos, was more steadfast than to the Mahomedans whom they served only as successors of the Beejapoor kings, and until the power of Hyder Ali arose, their local consequence was not diminished. In the perpetual wars between Hyder and the Mahrattas, in which the chief authority of the Beydur districts was sometimes in the hands of one, sometimes of the other, they fared very badly, being obliged to pay heavy contributions to both, which were enforced at the point of the sword. Hence their influence gradually declined, and many of the families became extinct. That of

Hurpunhullee had shared with that of Chittuldroog, the chief power and influence of the Beydurs; and, as nearest to Beejanuggur, was most trusted and most employed by Ali Adil Shah. In 1752 the chief submitted to Hyder Ali, and became a valuable and much trusted officer: and up to 1786 he preserved most part of his hereditary feudal territory, with his baronial rights. Whether Tippoo Sultan was tired of these Beydur chiefs or resented the antiquity of their families and privileges, and their local power, is not known; but Chittuldroog had previously fallen to his father, as will be separately explained, and his treatment of the Naïks of Hurpunhullee and Raidroog is thus recorded by Colonel Wilks:—

"On his return (that is, from the districts near and beyond the Tumboodra) by a route passing nearly "midway between Hurpunhullee and Raidroog, he made detachments, on pretence of dispersing his army in "cantonments, of two brigades, with secret instructions, to each of these fortresses; and having previously "removed all grounds of suspicion, by repeated personal acknowledgments to the Poligars of those places, for "the distinguished services they had rendered in the late campaign, he seized their chiefs and principal officers "in camp on the same day and hour as his brigades overpowered their unsuspecting garrisons. The cash and "effects of every kind, not excepting the personal ornaments of the women, were carried off as royal plunder, "and the chiefs were sent to the accustomed fate of Cabal Droog."

In his own memoirs the Sultan justifies the annexation of these dependencies to his dominions on the ground of the uncertain allegiance of the chiefs to his father, and their conspiracies in regard to himself; but there was in fact no real ground for the act, which was one of groundless and tyrannical spoliation and brutality. Even the Sultan's historian, Meer Hussein Ali Kirmáni, in his relation of the transaction, gives no reason for it, except that the Sultan "hated them."

The family of Hurpunhullee was not, however, extinguished, and in 1792 the oppression of Tippoo's local officers at Chittuldroog drove the Beydurs into rebellion, which was suppressed with much difficulty. After the fall of Seringapatam, the Hurpunhullee district formed part of those transferred to the Nizam, by whom the family was recognized, and to some extent reinstated; finally, in the cession of the country acquired from Tippoo south of the Krishna, to the British Government, Hurpunhullee was included, and belongs now to the Collectorate of Bellary. The family still exists, but is in reduced circumstances, subsisting upon a pension from the British Government and some ancestral hereditary lands.

THE Beydur family of Chittuldroog were of similar rank with that of Hurpunhullee, and other Beydur clans in the north of Mysore. They were feudal vassals of the kings of Beejanuggur, and had probably served as military dependants of the Bellâls, and before them of the Chalúkyas and Kadumbas. The family is unquestionably of very ancient origin. Taking advantage of the confusion which followed the destruction of Beejanuggur, the Naiks of Chittuldroog very considerably increased their territory, until it yielded a revenue, according to Dr. Buchanan, of 350,000 pagodas, or about 110,000*l.* a year. By these means the Naiks maintained their numerous clan, estimated at twelve thousand fighting men, in great efficiency, and became formidable local barons, as it were, levying black mail upon the country to a considerable distance. This was one of the families with whom settlements were made by Ali Adil Shah II; and the clan did excellent service for the Beejapoor state as long as it existed, in connection with the Beydur clans at Sugger, Hurpunhullee, and other Beydur baronies. On the reduction of Beejapoor, the Imperial troops endeavoured to gain possession of the territory of Chittuldroog; but the Naïk retreated to his fort, and no impression could be made upon him. A composition for a payment of tribute was effected, but it is very questionable whether the Beydur chiefs ever actually paid tribute to the Mahomedans: their great boast is that they never did. When the Mahrattas became possessed of the line of the Tumboodra as a frontier, they pressed the Beydur chiefs severely, and among others the Naik of Chittuldroog, who joined them on many occasions, though he never appears to have become entirely a Mahratta subject. Up to this time, and during the growth of the Mysoor state, the Beydur Naiks had preserved their independence; but as Hyder Ali attained power, he determined to bring these doubtful frontier chiefs to subjection, and in 1762, after his successful campaign against the Mahrattas of Gooty, advanced into the Beydur district. His summons was obeyed by the Naiks or Poligars of Raidroog and Hurpunhullee. The chief of Chittuldroog at first evaded attendance; but on his country being plundered by Hyder's cavalry, eventually made a merit of necessity, and visited him. No good will, however, was ever pretended by either, for the chief's heart was ever with the Mahrattas, whose Hindoo faith and predatory habits were more suited to wild Beydurs than the more civilized usages of a Mahomedan court. Hyder Ali was, however, content to bide his time; and nothing further occurred till 1776, by which time he had possessed himself of the country as far north as Bunkapoor. In this year he was threatened by a combined movement on the part of the Mahrattas and the Nizam, and summoned the Beydur clans among other dependants. To this summons the chief of Chittuldroog did not appear. He was negotiating at Poona, and trusted the Mahratta army would reach Mysoor in time to protect him, and receive his aid in reconquering the northern districts from Hyder. This, however, did not follow, and he had no resource but to await Hyder's attack, which was made as soon as troops could be collected. A memorable siege followed. The Beydurs, rash and brave to a proverb, did not fail in the severe trial; and their daily sorties, in which numbers of heads were carried off from the trenches and pickets, to be presented to the image of Kali in the fort, were hardly ever checked. This image of Kali has been an object of hereditary worship by the Chittuldroog clan from the earliest times. Kali or Parwutti, the wife of Vishnu, is the Kool Swámi, or household divinity, of the family; and to satisfy her craving for blood, the most precious being human sacrifice, the sorties on Mondays, which are sacred to the goddess, were especially the most memorable, and are thus quaintly recorded by Meer Hussein Ali Khan, Hyder Ali's biographer: "The beseiged," he says, "sallied out from the fort, and raised the confusion of the day of judgment among the guards and sentinels at "the batteries, and taking the heads of the slain, and tying them to a string, they hung them round their "necks, like red roses, and thus returned, and received rewards from their chiefs for the deeds they had done." Burma Naik, whose personal bravery was notorious, and had procured for him the soubriquet of Bich-Kutti, or "thrower away of the scabbard," defended his fort with such obstinate valour, that Hyder, after a heavy loss of men and matériel, and being again threatened by the Mahrattas, abandoned the siege, which had continued for three months, and retreated, but with the determination to recommence operations when a favourable opportunity should occur; and in 1778 he again invested the fort, with a larger army and more perfect matériel than before. The events of the second siege are almost a repetition of the first; but the offerings of heads to Kali were fewer, while the desperate efforts of the Beydurs to obtain them cost Burma Naïk his best kinsmen and clansmen. Eventually a body of three thousand Mahomedans in his service were corrupted by Hyder; and on hearing of their treachery, the old chieftain mounted his state palankeen, and ordered himself to be carried to Hyder's presence, where he submitted. He was henceforth a state prisoner for life, and all his family jewels and plate, with other property in the fort, became Hyder's booty. It was impossible, however, to break the spirit of the Beydur clan, which feared neither mutilation, torture, nor death; and Hyder, struck with their indomitable spirit, carried off nearly 20,000 of the adult males and boys to Seringapatam, where they formed the nucleus of his and his son's celebrated Chéla, or "disciple" infantry.

The treaty of 1790, between the British and the Peshwah, provided for the territories of the Beydur chiefs of Chittuldroog, Hurpunhullee, &c, being restored to them as dependants of the Mahratta state; but beyond a small pension, now paid by the British government, no restoration, except to freedom, was made: and on that allowance, and the enjoyment of some ancestral lands, the once powerful family of Chittuldroog now exists. It is nearly related to that of Sugger Shorapoor, which was the last Beyder family that preserved any independent existence as a state. Up to the year 1857-58, when the Rajah, having joined the southern Mahratta treasonable confederacy, rebelled, Shorapoor, in virtue of its existence as a principality, had become the head of the Beydur clans; but the family of Chittuldroog, if poor, has not relaxed in pride of birth, while traditions of the famous siege of Chittuldroog, and of the valiant deeds of Burma Bich-Kutti, and other warriors, are still sung by its bards, extending to the dim ages of the Pandus and Kurus, and the wars of the Rámáyun and Mahábhárut.